An Absolutely Ordinary Monday

By
Mary Anne Allen

Copyright © 2025 Mary Anne Allen

All rights reserved

No part of this publication may be reproduced, stored in a retrieval system, or transmitted in any form or by any means, electronic, mechanical, photocopying, recording, or otherwise, without prior written permission of the copyright owner, except in the case of brief quotations used in reviews or articles.

Dedication

For, Prof Geoffrey Herkes, without whom I would not be here my voiceless inmates in 7F Mrs Purdy, who gave me the confidence to write in the first place and most of all my dearest Mum and Dad and my children, Adelaide and Alex.

Acknowledgment

Thank you to everyone who encouraged me on my journey to write this book and bring words to the printed page.

Special thanks to Mum and Dad, who always believed in me, and to Mrs. Purdy, my Year 10 English teacher, who once told me that Harper Lee would one day have to move over for me.

Thank you to Sandra, Sue, Susie, Wendy, Rose Marie, and Maureen for their invaluable feedback, and to the Austen Group for sharing their thoughtful insights.

A very special thank you to Delle for sharing her gift of art.

Thank you to Lilly and her team of editors, publishers, and web designers.

And finally, thank you to you, for reading my story.

Table of Contents

Dedication iii

Acknowledgment iv

Introducing… Me 1

Incomplete Paraplegic 4

An Absolutely Ordinary Day 10

Rollercoaster 21

Dead Leg 26

Emergency Department 34

MRI 40

Needles 47

Meet The Prof. 54

Going for a Walk 64

What Difference a View Makes 70

After the Big Toe 77

The Visits 96

Moving Day 103

The Breakout 111

Mt Wilga 118

Down the Aisle 138

Just Popping In 147

Music 152

Contact With The Outside 160

Shopping Expedition 181

Driver's Licence 187

Losing My Independence 192

Residuals 195

The Big Long Sigh 204

My Fight Song 210

Introducing... Me

I am a Mum. I am a Mum to 14-year-old twins. Their names are Adelaide Grace and Alex Michael. They are my most enormous pride and joy, and my greatest loves. Before they were born, I had no idea how much I could possibly love someone. I loved my parents and siblings and husband, of course. But I discovered that loving my children was a completely different story.

I am a Daughter. That probably should come first, because I was a daughter before I was a mother. My parents were my first teachers and my first loves. They were the first people who showed me how to relate to others and taught me the lessons of life. They shared their wisdom through their words, their actions, their faith and their soul. I am the person I am because of them. I have missed them every day since they left this earth. I look for signs of them in the air and the world around me. People say a feather can be a sign, or music can be a sign. Every now and again, I see them in Adelaide's raised eyebrow or in Alex's comments about the world. It's not the same as being able to hold them and hug them. I am still a daughter, but a daughter who feels lost.

I am a Sister. I am the oldest Sister. Of seven children. Of eight, actually. Timothy was born alive but had the umbilical cord around his neck. It's awful that the very thing that kept him joined to Mum, giving him life for all those months, was the same thing that took his life. I take my role as Sister, as oldest Sister, very seriously. I have always tried to do whatever I could for my siblings. It sadly hasn't always been what they wanted.

I am a Teacher. The first time I was ever asked, 'What do you want to be when you grow up?' I was about five years old. I was in kindergarten. It's a silly question to ask a child. The world is our oyster, and so many of the roles we are preparing children for don't even exist yet. It was a different world with a different mindset in 1976. So I was asked the question. I had been at school for about a week.

I answered with gusto: 'I'm going to be a ballerina.'

Where had that come from? Ballerinas were not really big in the world of five-year-olds in Windsor in 1976! Windsor was a semi-rural town about 90 minutes north-west of Sydney. It's closer to Sydney now because the roads are much better and the cars are faster. It's not really semi-rural any more; it's on the fringes of semi-rural. There were certainly no ballerinas pirouetting through town on a regular basis.

It was when I was in Year One that I knew I was going to be a Teacher. That thought never wavered. Even when I was encouraged by teachers to do something else. I studied hard, worked hard and loved my job with a passion. Even when not in a formal teaching role in a school, I find great joy in teaching others. I really believe it's a calling.

I am an ex-Wife. For sixteen years I was a Wife. I was the one who made the call to walk away. It was the best call for both of us. I was so in love with Mike when we got married.

Our wedding day was the happiest I could ever imagine, until our babies were born. Then that day took over. I tried to do everything I could to make Mike happy. In the end, I knew neither of us was, and I knew it was best for both of us—and for Alex and Adelaide—to try to be happy apart. I could never have dreamt how that could have all blown up and had the opposite effect. There was such spite and contempt. Our world suffered a true nuclear explosion, the effects of which I fear will go on forever.

Mum. Daughter. Sister. Teacher. Ex-Wife. These are only a few of the parts that make up me. Parishioner. Voter. Creator. Explorer. Manager. Thinker. Citizen. There are so many more. They all have capital letters because they are all so important.

Incomplete Paraplegic

I am an Incomplete Paraplegic.

It has taken me a long time to be able to accept this label. To own that this is truly mine. You see, I don't like it. I don't want it.

Would anyone?

Paralysis: noun. Paralysis occurs when you're unable to make voluntary muscle movements. A nervous system problem causes paralysis. Nerves send signals to your muscles. Those signals make your muscles move. When you're paralysed, or have paralysis, you can't move certain areas of your body.

Paralysis can affect any part of your body. https://my.clevelandclinic.org/health/diseases/15345-paralysis

Incomplete: adjective. An incomplete injury means that the ability of the spinal cord to convey messages to or from the brain is not entirely lost.

Additionally, some sensation (even if it's feint) and movement is possible below the level of injury.https://www.christopherreeve.org/todays-care/living-with-paralysis/newly-paralyzed/how-is-an-sci-defined-and-what-is-a-complete-vs-incomplete-injury/

For me, Incomplete Paraplegia began at 11:15 am on 15th July 2013. Exactly 11 years, 11 months and 26 days, or 626 weeks ago.

4379 days or 105,094 hours. 6,305,680 minutes or 22.64% of my life has been spent as an Incomplete Paraplegic. Some people have catastrophic, life-altering events happen to them and stoically announce to the masses, 'I wouldn't change it for the world.'

I heard a very famous paralympian once say, 'I'm glad my disability happened to me.'

Well, just as stoically and just as bravely, I announce, 'I would give almost anything to change it.' And, 'I most certainly am not glad that my disability happened to me.' To tell you the truth, I hate it. I hate that this happened to my body. I was fitter than I had ever been: healthy, playing and running with my children, free of melanoma. Well. It hit me out of nowhere like a lightning bolt. There was no warning. No accident or injury. This was an illness out of the blue. An auto-immune reaction to who-knows-what which sent my body into overdrive.

Most spinal cord injuries are readily explained by a traumatic accident or injury. Maybe a car crash or a motorbike accident. Perhaps a tackle gone wrong in a football match. The 2020–21 Census recorded 53% of spinal hospitalisations for males (www.aihw.gov.au). When most people think of someone who is 'paralysed,' they think of someone in a wheelchair who simply can't move their legs. Many people assume that if I can move the lower half of my body, I'm a fraud. A car full of little old ladies on their way to a funeral saw me getting Alex and Adelaide out of the car in the blue wheelchair spot to go to their swimming lessons one morning. We had all the usual swimming gear: goggles, towels, change of clothes, undies, shoes, kickboard, snacks. Times two. I was balancing all of that, holding hands so no one would get run over, and trying to walk across gum nuts to get to the pool on time. The driver wound her window down, slowed her gold Mercedes, placed her head near the window so the breeze just gently swished her purple rinse, and yelled out, 'Leave those parking spots for people who really need them!' I wonder if she would've reacted the same if the person wrangling the swimming gear — me — was in a wheelchair? A complete paraplegic. Probably not.

I was ignorant of truly understanding what it meant to be Paraplegic. I never comprehended the full extent of consequences for inside and outside the body. The pressure on all the body systems never crossed my mind. Was I ignorant? Or was this simply something that was not in my field of view? I just didn't need to know it.

So I am an Incomplete Paraplegic — in capital letters because it is undeniably important in my life. It has been my life for almost a quarter of it.

Why Am I Speaking Out?

In Year 12, I studied the poetry of Les Murray. I was fortunate to be able to meet Mr Les Murray. The teachers organised an incursion where the students studying his poetry went into the school hall and listened to him talk for an hour and a half.

He was the same age as my Dad. Born in 1938, at the beginning of World War II. He was a large man with a strong presence. He was a country boy, born in Nabiac near Taree, and the flavour of his works was peppered with Aussie country. He often made comparisons between bush and city:

When Sydney and the Bush first met

There was no open ground

And men and girls, in chains and not,

All made an urgent sound.

(Sydney and the Bush, 1977)

There were some of us who were interested in hearing Mr Murray because he had written brilliant poetry. These people loved the imagery and loved the feelings that were evoked. These students wanted to know how he came up with his ideas and how he stitched them together. Why he thought poetry was still relevant. If he thought poetry was still relevant. This was the year before Les Murray was named one of the 100 Australian Living Treasures by the National Trust of Australia. Imagine being called a Living Treasure.

These people were the ones who wanted to know how this giant of a man could wrap these giant ideas in these tiny little words and still choose to live in a small country town after living in the massive world cities that he had lived in.

There were others of us who were interested because they wanted to squeeze information out of him like a damp kitchen sponge to get better grades. Those were the students who didn't care about learning, they just cared about the marks. You know the ones who walked into the exam hall, put out their pens and their alarm clock, taking no care for the people around them, setting the alarm for 30 minutes before the end, 15 minutes before the end and again 5 minutes before the end. They weren't really interested in the deeper meaning of the poetry or of the man in front of them, they just wanted to know about the test questions. These were the people that killed the poetry.

And of course, there were some who were simply not interested. What a waste of time for them. They just did not care.

I would like to say that my main motivation was the first reason, the most noble. And it partly was. But it was also partly the second. I wanted to do well. I always tried to do well, always pushed myself to do the best I could. And if I could beat the other people around me, even better! I was very competitive!

He looked like a lot of our dads: bald, ageing, glasses in his top pocket ready. A briefcase down beside his leg.

The glasses came out of the top pocket and perched on the end of his nose. They didn't really seem to fit his head properly, they sat above the tops of his ears. He looked down his nose, through the lenses and over the top at us. The book in his hand was dwarfed by his bulk.

Then Les Murray began to speak.

He sat on a chair in front of us, the ragtag crew of pimply-faced students stared.

I came away spellbound. To this day, I remember what he said.

'Poetry is about emotions. Emotions are the edge of language.'

Emotions are the edge of language.

Much of what has happened to me since 15th July 2013 has been sitting right on the edge of comprehension and, for so many people, especially the inmates of Ward 7F, on the edge of language. I am one of the lucky ones who has the language, the voice to describe what happened.

> *Longing for tears as children for a rainbow –*
> *And many weep for sheer acceptance, and more*
> *Refuse to weep for fear of all acceptance,*
> *Not words, but grief, not messages, but sorrow,*

(An Absolutely Ordinary Rainbow, 1969)

I need to use my language, my voice, for those who can't.

An Absolutely Ordinary Day

Les Murray wrote a poem *"An Absolutely Ordinary Rainbow."* This particular day was the beginning of anything but ordinary.

The ordinary Mondays were precious. Mondays belonged to Mum and Dad. Monday was sacred. I would not make plans and Mum and Dad would not make plans. We spent our Mondays together. We never did anything remarkable, rather the extraordinary was in the ordinary, in the expected.

It was too difficult to get to Mass on Sunday morning. Just Alex, Adelaide and me. I'm talking about 2013 when my babies were only two. St Michaels was a large church with a big congregation and quite a lot of tut-tutting if children made a sound at the wrong time. We used to arrive with a giant pencil case for each child, with a few different things to keep them busy: a book to read, a little puzzle of the Disney princesses, a calculator with large buttons – Adelaide's was lolly pink and Alex's was sky blue, a notebook and coloured pencils. They knew they weren't allowed to take out their goodies until after the Gospel.

It must have looked funny to watch. 'The Gospel of the Lord,' announced the Priest.

When the congregation replied, 'Praise to you, Lord Jesus Christ,' my two little bodies bobbed down to the floor, unzipped their giant bags and pulled out their favourite things that day. They kept busy with their own choices, every now and again craning their necks to see what the other was doing, just in case they were missing something interesting.

Then, at the 'Our Father,' their little heads popped up again. They stood bolt upright and we held each other's hands. They knew the way things worked. They knew the pattern of when to sit and when to stand.

At Communion they joined the queue for their special blessing, with their arms across their chests to show they were not able to receive the Eucharist. They knew what to do. 'Jesus loves you.'

The first 'Amen' came loud and clear. And then the next.

Then straight back under the seats for the puzzle and the calculator. But sometimes the bag of tricks just wasn't enough distraction.

One Sunday I got so upset with the evil eyes from the two old ladies in front of us and the whispering and the tongue clicking, that I grabbed Adelaide and Alex by the hand and stormed out. I was so upset I took us outside. The hot angry tears burned the back of my eyes and down the inside of my throat and if anyone had spoken to me I would have exploded. But they didn't. They just stared and judged. We three were on our own in that crowd in that Holy Space. No one bothered.

We went out, but we didn't leave. We had every right to be there. We had as much right as the eyes that were rolling at us. I waited until the end of Mass when the two pious women came out looking very pleased with themselves for cleansing the church of such riff-raff.

'Perhaps next time rather than ridiculing, you could ask if I need help. You don't know what it takes for me to get us here. You don't know how easy it would be for us not to come.'

They both just glared at me. Both of them in their Sunday best. And me in my mumsy clothes with mushy toast smeared on them. I felt tiny beside them, but at least I used my voice. I felt stronger for that.

'I hope you both have a lovely day,' I said to them as they went on their merry way.

I took Alex and Adelaide back into the church to pack up our things. We passed Father on our way. 'We were basically chased out,' I told him with a voice still ready to break.

'Well. People come to hear Mass. What can you expect?' I was so upset and so disappointed by the reaction of the man who was the priest at the time. When we got to the car, I stared out the windscreen. How can you respond to that?

Interestingly, one of the ladies, Anna, became one of our closest acquaintances at St Michaels. She brought little treats and notes for Adelaide and Alex as they got older and always stopped and spoke to us. I like to hope that those two women and any other adults who heard me went away that day and thought about what they were really doing, living life as a Catholic. Anna showed at a very simple level that maybe it was more than just sitting in a pew.

Because it was so hard to get to and through the big Sunday Mass at St Michaels, I would take my two-year-olds to Mass at Mary Help of Christians Chapel at Greenwich on Monday morning with Father George. Mary Help of Christians is part of the wider St Michaels Parish but quite separate. It's an Independent Living place for retirees. It's the sort of place I thought would be perfect for Mum and Dad: not too big, private but with other people if they wanted company, a little shop across the road, an inbuilt chapel. And it was close to us at Lane Cove.

Father George adored Alex and Adelaide. They walked down the little aisle to get their special blessing on their forehead and he gladly made the sign of the cross for them. They stood in front of him with their little arms crossed over their chests with their heads bowed. They knew what to do. And when they heard, 'Jesus loves you,' they heartily answered 'Amen,' and walked back to their place. Renewed for the week. Or at least a few minutes!

At the end of Mass, Fr George and the old parishioners milled around and made a fuss. They made us feel welcome. No tutting, no eye rolling and no tongue clicking. I wished Mum and Dad could live there. Dad would love the community aspect of it. He became very social after his retirement. Mum would love the closeness to her grandchildren. The social side would exhaust Mum, she was very good at it but it was draining for her.

Every Monday – after Mass when I could get us there – Mum and Dad would arrive with their chicken from Woolworths and any other things they thought we needed. And then it all began. Our ordinariness.

'Hello. Who's there?' we heard from beyond the front door. Always the same cheerful voice. Always Dad. 'Hello. Who is it?' From outside. Odd, really. Usually the people on the inside of the door ask that question, but on Mondays, at our place, the 'who is it?' came from outside the door. Every week. And we always had to guess who it could possibly be.

Always the sound of walking sticks tapping down the front steps towards the door. Always Mum. Those steps were treacherous. Mum was slower. We were all terrified of those steps. There was nothing to hold onto, nothing for support. My heart leapt into my throat each time I heard those sticks for fear the owner of them might tumble down the steep stairs and land on the rocks below.

From inside the house, always four little feet tearing around to see which body would reach the door first. Always Alex and Adelaide racing to the door to see who was outside – like it would ever change. It never did. It was an Absolutely Ordinary Monday.

It was the same at the start of every week. It was Dad carrying the black and grey floral insulated picnic bag holding the Woolies BBQ chicken that he chose because

'They're better value than the chickens at Red Rooster. And they taste better than the chicken at KFC.' He always reckoned those were dry. As kids we used to hope that Dad's beloved Parramatta would make it into the NRL Grand Final because we made a deal with him that we would get KFC for dinner. It didn't happen very often! I think he preferred the Woolworths chooks because they were usually cheaper.

There were often the little sprinkle cupcakes that Mum chose because she knew Alex liked the pink icing and Adelaide liked the chocolate icing, and they were treats that I never bought. There were other things too: a few potatoes or a cauliflower that Dad's brother had grown, or a loaf of bread just because.

Dad also came armed with his drill and toolbox to help us repair things around the place. There was always something that needed fixing.

One Monday, Dad came prepared with little knobs to drill onto the drawers and cupboards in the kitchen. Our kitchen was in such a state that it really ought to have been condemned. It couldn't be fixed because I was afraid of pulling bits down to fix it and finding things like asbestos or lead and ending up with a bigger problem than knob-less drawers and cupboards. On one of Dad's walks around the neighbourhood which were prescribed by his cardiologist, he passed a bathroom vanity put out on the side of the road for council clean-up. 'I liked those knobs,' he told me. But he also said the vanity was in such pristine condition it would be a shame to take it apart. 'Someone might need it. So I just left it and waited.'

When the vanity was still there on his next walk and the walk after that, he decided no one was going to use it, so he unscrewed the handles and brought them to us. I wonder if the council workers noticed that the little handles were all missing? I wonder if they thought a thief might have passed in the night? They never could have known the joy that knob-thief brought to my little family.

On this particular Ordinary Monday, Dad opened his toolbox and out rolled a veritable treasure chest of shining white curved knobs and sparkling silver screws to go with them. As they scattered across the table with the greatest fanfare Dad could muster, they were met with the heartiest oohs and aahs we could bellow!

With his trusty little helpers, Adelaide wearing her apron and Alex with his tool belt of timber tools strapped on, Dad went straight to work breathing life into our kitchen drawers and cupboards. We all stood back and admired the handiwork of the three and showed enormous gratitude for the improvement these little gems from the roadside collection made to our lives. No more splinters under our fingernails trying to prise open doors to get to our plates, no more wobbling doors to get them to open. No more paint flaking off every time we needed to open a drawer for a spoon, revealing yet another layer of aged paint beneath. We felt like we had a new kitchen. We still had crooked doors and missing pieces. But we had knobs! And Grandad was as proud as punch that he could deliver.

A few years later I was searching for a birthday card for Dad, on the $2 card stand in the newsagent. Alex – about six at the time – came running down the aisle waving something, (which was unusual because they knew they weren't supposed to touch anything). 'Mum! Mum! This is it! This is the perfect card for Grandad!' And I looked at the $12.99 handmade card wrapped in plastic that said Happy Birthday in handwritten cursive. I looked at the price. My eyes widened and I almost dropped it in case my plebeian fingers marked the goods. My first thought was, 'I am not paying $13 for a birthday card! It might as well be made of gold!' But when I turned it over and saw the tiny little fairy-sized screwdriver, saw, pliers and hammer all cut out and pegged onto a wispy little piece of silver line above a fairy-sized toolbox that looked just like Dad's, and I looked at Alex's proud Grandad-loving face, we walked out of that store with what is probably the most expensive card I have ever bought! Dad loved it. And Mum nearly cried.

Mum came prepared on our ordinary Mondays too. She made sure she wore great big, bright flowers. Purples or oranges or greens or blues. And she wore beads that tiny baby fingers could play with, or chew. And then as the little babies grew older, the beads were transferred from Mama to toddler, like an Olympic gold medal.

Mum never had fancy or expensive jewellery. She had a simple gold cross that her sister Rewa gave her when she was her bridesmaid in 1969 and her wedding ring and engagement ring. That gold cross, the size of her thumbnail, meant everything to Mum. She was always so close to her sister. They lived so far apart: Windsor to Mackay in the days before mobile phones meant calls were costly, so in our house, long-distance calls were rare. But Mum and Rewa seemed to have some kind of telepathy, where they almost knew when they were going to call each other. It was uncanny. Mum was devastated when Aunty Rewa died in 1994 at only 47. The gold cross meant even more then. It meant she still carried part of her sister with her. She went from sometimes wearing the cross, to wearing it almost every day.

Until it was stolen. Along with Mum's other treasured piece of jewellery, her engagement ring.

One scorching day, Mum's fingers were swollen, it was too hot to wear jewellery, so Mum left her precious gold cross and her beloved engagement ring on the bathroom window ledge. Someone else, some stranger with no connection to Mum or Dad, decided that they had more of a claim over two of Mum's three most valuable possessions. So they took them. Dad searched every second-hand or pawn shop within what he thought was a reasonable distance and within a reasonable time. But nothing. Dad gave Mum his mother's engagement ring, which his older brother had. It was a thoughtful gesture, but it was never the same for Mum. It was never truly hers.

After that, any jewellery that Mum had was precious because it was chosen for its 'playability,' or how well it could be used to play with her grandchildren. And Mum was an expert at choosing things for their playability!

How bright was it?

How glittery was it?

How chunky was it?

Did it have an unusual feel?

Could you use it to tell a story?

Was there a memory linked to it?

Could you use it to create a memory?

Could it be taken off and borrowed for the duration of a visit without little people worrying about whether they might break it?

Was it made by someone she knew? Those preschool macaroni and wool necklaces were priceless.

I got to share the loves of my life with the other loves of my life. I got to watch them learn from each other. I got to see Adelaide and Alex love Mum and Dad in the way that you just love someone. No reasons, you just love them. And I got to see Mum and Dad love Alex and Adelaide in the same way.

It's like the love does a full circle.

Perhaps more of a spiral, because in a circle it would just keep spinning around as Kylie Minogue so cheekily says in one of her little dance ditties.

But the love doesn't keep spinning endlessly, it shifts and evolves. Those ordinary Mondays showed me how love changes as we change. Mum and Dad were different as grandparents than they were as parents.

Happier almost. More free. More at ease.

And my children were different as grandchildren than they were as children. More gentle somehow.

And I got to be a go-between. I always said to Mum, from before my children were born, that if I could help it, I didn't want to rely on Mum and Dad for childcare, because I knew it would alter the relationship between them. I wanted it to be just as it was on those Ordinary Mondays.

The Ordinary Mondays were extraordinary.

Extraordinary in their ordinariness.

The Absolutely Ordinary Mondays.

Rollercoaster

Ours was a square dinner table. It wore a grey plastic tablecloth with white spots, so it was easy to wipe clean. I had some lovely tablecloths too. A beautiful white lace one that I carted back from Murano, and a bright yellow one that came from Provence. But two-year-old mealtimes could be a bit like a Pro Hart painting, so the grey plastic tablecloth with the felt backing from Hot Dollar down the road was much more practical.

Alex and Adelaide sat opposite each other on Ikea high chairs without the trays. That's how I made sure they were part of the family at mealtimes. They could reach everything, they could see everything, and they could share in the conversation. Alex, Adelaide, Mike and I were a family of four. Lots of families had the children eat first and the parents eat later, once the children were asleep. I tried to make sure we all broke bread together. Mealtimes were communal.

It was the same on our Absolutely Ordinary Mondays. Adelaide and Alex sat opposite each other, Mum and Dad opposite each other. It was like a circle but at a square table. That way everyone could see and hear each other. No one felt more or less important because there was no head of the table. It was our King Arthur's Square Table. I kind of floated between the table and the kitchen.

The Woolworths chicken was warm, that was the highlight. There were usually boiled eggs or even scrambled eggs.

Sometimes homemade coleslaw or iceberg lettuce and tomato. Always grated tasty cheese and soft bread rolls because grandparents' teeth and two-year-old teeth preferred soft things! There were knives and forks for Mum and Dad, forks and spoons for Alex and Adelaide, and water was the drink of choice for all of us. Sometimes we even lashed out and had something fancy like tinned pineapple rings.

On 15 July 2013, the four of us sat down at the table. Dad in his blue flannelette shirt, Mum in her big purple flowers and beads. They were so happy to be with us, and we were so happy to be with them. We shared our lunch and, as always, Alex and Adelaide finished first. They got up to play and I started to clear the leftovers and the dirty plates.

'I'll just wash up,' I shouted from the kitchen. I could hear the chatter between grandparents and grandchildren. The sounds made me smile into the dish bubbles.

I finished and joined Mum at the table. With my back to the wall, I could see the whole room: Dad sinking into the lounge, starting to drift off to sleep; Alex playing with Lego on the floor; and Adelaide using the pencils and papers next to him. The room had that after-lunch contentment. My phone rang from the bedroom. It was a tiny house, two bedrooms, so the phone was only a few steps away down the hall. I stood up from the wooden chair, pushed out from the table and stretched my legs.

It was the calm before the storm, like sitting on a roller coaster waiting for the start. I'm not a fan of roller coasters.

I went to Australia's Wonderland with my friend Karen when I was 18, the summer after our Year 12 exams. Karen worked at Wonderland, like so many of the teens who lived around my high school. There were two roller coaster options: the Big Beastie, which was on metal tracks, and the Baby Beastie, on wooden tracks. We went on the Baby Beastie. It was my first time on a roller coaster and after I rode it, I vowed it would be my last!

Karen and I sat at the very front. We waited and, even though we weren't moving, my stomach started to lurch and twist into knots. I hung onto the rail in front of me so tight it's a wonder I didn't leave imprints. We took off, slowly at first. That was fine — we were on the flat. But I could tell I was going to regret the decision to get on board. We clickety-clacked up a steep climb after a couple of metres. My heart slowed down to almost nothing, my face turned cold, but my armpits started to sweat. I could see the top.

Then I couldn't see anything. We reached the crescendo. Everything paused: the Beastie, the sweat, my heart. Then, ever so slowly, we took the dive over the edge. That move took forever. The sweat poured like a torrent. My heart was a raging thunderstorm. My ears pounded. My screams were sounds I didn't know I could make — high-pitched, constant, blood-curdling.

Lucky for me, my eyes were as wide as my mouth, which made it easier not to miss any of the death-defying bends and dips. I was sure as we hurtled and rattled, up, down, round and round, that we would surely die. I believed my screaming would signal the end of Karen and me, and that gripping that rail would do us no good. I opened my mouth at the top of that rickety rise. Karen waved her arms and laughed and carried on as though she actually enjoyed herself. How dare she risk our lives like that? How could I ever forgive her? Our bodies pounded from side to side and the shaking was unbearable.

I didn't close my mouth again until we slowed down at the station. It was either the end of the ride or the end of our lives. I wasn't sure. I climbed out of that carriage and jumped onto the platform so fast I'm sure I set a record, shaking violently like an earthquake.

How can that be called fun? It was fun for Karen, she kept looking at me and laughing. She thought I was hilarious. She didn't understand the pure fear and terror coursing through my body. Friends shouldn't do that to each other. She took me there. She said we'd have fun. She called it an 'amusement park!' She worked there! She knew how death-defying the ride was. How could she put me on it? How could I bow to peer pressure and agree to risk life and limb? What was I thinking?

Stupid decision. I should have stuck to the dodgem cars!

When I stood up from our shared table, it was very much like being at the top of that first dreaded rise of the roller coaster, after the calm flat part. Sitting at the top where you're looking over the edge into the abyss, when everything is suspended for what feels like a lifetime. Nothing works. Because nothing feels right. You know you're just about to start sweating and screaming. Your heart has stopped but it's just about to pop out of your chest.

That's what it was like. And it all happened in the space of a minute.

At 11:15 am.

Dead Leg

Remember what it was like to sit on your foot? You'd stand up and wobble all over the place. That's what happened. My left leg, from the ankle down, was elastic: it sprung backwards and forwards. I could stand up, but I really had to concentrate to have any semblance of control. *Lift that foot. Put that foot down. Bend that ankle. Move that foot forward. Leave that foot behind.* The foot was asleep. Or was it dead? I could tell it was different to when I sat on it during school assembly. I couldn't just shake it awake. It was a dead weight. The more I tried to shake it, the worse it got. And the worse it got, the further up my body it travelled.

'Mum, I think there's something wrong with my foot.' I was never one to make a fuss. In hindsight, I should've screamed, *There's something wrong with my body!* But what I said was like a whisper, not to panic anyone. Maybe not to panic myself.

'What do you mean?'

'I can't lift it without telling it what to do.' Again, in hindsight, I should have screamed and cried, *My leg is dead!* I should have panicked. It would have been fair to cause everyone around me to panic. Of course, hindsight is a great thing.

The word **STROKE** was circling around my mind, but now it was coming closer to the front. It was like one of those baby mobiles that spin gently in the breeze. *Don't think of the word and it will go away.*

STROKE

Don't think the word. **STROKE**

Don't think it. **STROKE**

If you say it out loud it might happen. **STROKE**

Just. Don't. Say. It.

I didn't say it out loud. Mum didn't say it out loud, and neither did Dad. We didn't even whisper it. It was like there were two sides of my brain talking to me, starting to argue:

'It looks and sounds and feels like you're having a stroke.'

'No. Don't be ridiculous. You can't be having a stroke. Don't even think it.'

'If you're having a stroke, you need to do something about it early.'

'If you pretend nothing is wrong, it will go away.'

'If you don't do anything about it, you could die. Or worse.'

'You're too young.'

You're too frightened.

You've got too much to lose.

This is not the way the ordinary goes.

'Call the Health Line.' Mum was always very wise and matter of fact.

The nurse on the other end of the Health Line was very efficient as she worked through her checklist. 'Can you breathe? Have you lost consciousness? Are you in pain? Describe what is happening.'

'Yes, I can breathe. No, I haven't lost consciousness. No, I'm not in pain. It just feels like I have pins and needles and numbness in my foot. Actually, it started in my foot, but when I stood up it travelled to my knee. Now when I try to lift my foot and when I try to walk, I can't. I have to concentrate and tell myself what to do. I don't have any real control over my foot or the bottom of my left leg.'

'It sounds like you're having a stroke. It sounds like you need an ambulance.'

Just like that, the word was let loose. It was out in the open.

STROKE

'I can't go in an ambulance. I have two babies. They need me. I think I'll call my doctor.'

'That's up to you. Remember, if it is a stroke, the quicker we deal with it, the better the outcome.'

I thanked her and called my doctor.

'No, I'm afraid she is busy all day. There are no appointments with Dr MacDonald.'

Do you think the receptionists understand the power they wield? I did something I would never usually do, I pulled out the big guns. 'The lady on the Health Line wondered if I could be having a stroke? I really need to talk to the doctor.'

'Well, it sounds like you need an ambulance. I'll try to get the doctor to give you a call in her lunch break.'

It sounded like a long wait, but it really wasn't. By now it was about 1:00.

'It sounds like you could be having a stroke. I'll have to order tests, but I can't do that until later this afternoon. I think you'd be better off with an ambulance, going straight to hospital.'

I didn't bother with an appointment. I didn't bother with that doctor. I haven't seen her again. I have since found a wonderful GP who has been with me for years.

I spoke to Mum and Dad. The leg wasn't getting any better. Now it was dead up to my knee. I walked up the 26 steps to the letterbox - just to make sure the whole thing wasn't in my imagination.

It wasn't. I walked back down to the house, dragging the left leg.

Then - just to make sure - I walked down the back steps, another 26, and put washing in the machine. There was still work to do. I talked to Mum and Dad about what the Health Line nurse and the doctor said. I couldn't think of any other serious options. I just couldn't. It wasn't getting any better. In fact, it was getting worse.

'If I put Alex and Adelaide down for their afternoon sleep, would you mind staying with them while I go to the hospital and get checked out? Then when I come back, you can go home? They'll sleep for about an hour and a half. That should be plenty of time.'

I kissed Alex and Adelaide and put them to bed.

The best-laid plans.

I called 000.

We waited.

And waited. The 20 minutes felt like an age. Mum's face showed worry lines. She didn't say much, she never did. I knew Dad was tossing things over in his mind, he would normally be asleep on the lounge by now. Instead, he was pacing the lounge room.

I packed my backpack with my wallet, phone and keys. I didn't think I'd need anything else. I intended to be back by the afternoon. By now it was just before 2:00. Sleep time.

We waited.

Finally, the ambulance arrived. Gary, with the square glasses and the friendly face, and Craig came to the door. It was

Gary who carried the black medical bag. They both automatically looked at Mum, as though she was the one who needed their help. Then Dad. They passed these looks in seconds. 'No, it's me,' I said, as we all had a little giggle and I headed for the door. Me with my one and a quarter working legs. There was no time to waste. I had to be back before the end of the afternoon sleep.

Gary and Craig checked me over. I explained to them about the heavy foot and the numb leg. I could still stand, and I could still walk. It looked like there was nothing wrong with me. I knew there had to be something. But no matter what, I would not say the word out loud.

Stroke.

Sleep time had always been a bit of a nightmare. My babies never wanted to sleep. There was just too much to miss out on. Before she was even born, Adelaide never kept still. There were arms and legs thumping me internally from north, south, east and west, not to mention directions that had never even been invented! She practised cartwheels with the skill of an Olympian. Her diagnosis of ADHD was really no surprise. Getting her to sleep took artistry, patience and love.

Adelaide asked me once, 'Who is the lady in the white dress that visits me at night time?' I'm sure there were women from generations past who knew how challenging things could be, who came to visit us to help. The lady in the white dress who appeared in the night was friendly and helpful at sleep time. Not scary at all. Someone who had been through it all before.

One night we were having a particularly tricky time. Adelaide and Alex were having a great time but not wanting to sleep. Their light started to flicker. I was upset so I announced, 'If you're not going to help, please, please just go away. And don't bother coming back.' So the flickering light stopped, and the lady in the white dress at night was never mentioned again.

Alex had the eyes of a wise old man from the day he was born. Four weeks early, he was like a man who'd lived for a hundred years. Even the photos of Alex as a brand-new baby, before his eyelashes had grown, showed him looking at Adelaide or me with those eyes and that serious face. He knew things. He always carried a calmness and a knowingness. Nothing has changed, except he's grown eyelashes. His mind worked so hard. No wonder he couldn't sleep. He was always thinking.

When they finally got to sleep, I had to be quick. Alex and Adelaide would be awake before we knew it, and Mum and Dad would be run off their feet. The afternoons were busy. I usually took them for a walk to Lane Cove and to the park on the way home. About 6 km for me, and a race, a swing, a kick of the ball and a climb of whatever we could for Alex and Adelaide. They would have afternoon tea in the pram and we'd chatter the whole way: 'Who can see the silver car?' 'Oh look, three buses in a row.' 'What a beautiful day, hardly any clouds at all.' And we'd natter on and on. This was July so it was winter. The sun would start to go down early and I didn't want Mum and Dad driving in the dark or getting caught in the horrible afternoon peak traffic.

I didn't have much time.

I don't know if Mum and Dad were more worried about me going off in the ambulance or about Adelaide and Alex waking up.

They're gone now. I'll never be able to ask them.

Emergency Department

People must be paid a lot of money to come up with fancy names for all the different variations of white or grey, Lexicon, Antique White, Natural White, Vivid White, Snow White, just so we can browse the aisles of Bunnings every weekend and collect the little swatches. We stand there, shoulder to shoulder with other people, all confused about the spectrum of one colour, wondering what it will look like in our light, in our corner, on our wall. Thinking about the ambience it will create in our space and if it will be the right tone for this year's look. None of us really knows, so we all line up to buy the genius little tester pots of paint. What a great idea they are. 'Ooh, I can't decide on one version of white, so I'll buy four!'

We, the weekend painters, take our swatches and our tester pots home and blu-tac little bits of white all over the walls in different parts of the house to catch light at different times of the day. Does it work? Do these strategies help? Sometimes, perhaps. Or sometimes do we just defer to Jim from AAA Painters in his paint-stained navy overalls, who has been doing the job for 30 years? 'Lexicon quarter strength is the best.' So that's what we go with. After all, Jim knows best.

Hospital Emergency Departments are that clinical grey, aren't they? Almost white, but not quite. Almost grey, but not quite. Sort of somewhere in between. Not really beige, that's got a different feel to it. I wonder if they ever ask AAA Jim for advice? These departments are a nothing colour, really. Perhaps it's not the fault of the paint, maybe it's a lighting problem. Those fluorescent lighting tubes that hum and give off that almost radioactive brightness. Maybe that's the problem. Whoever painted those walls didn't stand shoulder to shoulder with the Bunnings Brigade staring at the swatches and the sample pots. Nope, they just went for it.

Then there are the curtains around the examination cubicles. They try for a splash of colour: thick stripes of bright yellows and oranges. The colour researcher thinks the blandness of the walls needs the brightness of the curtains to make the place okay. These curtains in the Emergency Ward are bright, sunshiny colours, but they don't hide that smell of sickness. That smell of hand sanitiser we all got so used to during Covid.

And they don't hide the terrified, beady eyes. They don't hide the eyes resigned to sickness. The very frail old men and the tired old women, with ankles too skinny to hold their sagging bodies and eyes so sunken they can't see the world past those curtains any more. How is it they look like they've spent a lifetime there?

On 15 July 2013, my chauffeur-driven ambulance pulled into the Royal North Shore Emergency Department. One of the busiest hospitals in Australia. I was an insignificant no one, one of over 85,000 no ones that year to visit the Emergency Department. But to me and to my family, I was someone. I was Mum, I was daughter and sister and wife. Those bland walls and those sickly bright curtains welcomed me when I needed to visit. I didn't have those terrified, beady eyes or the skinny ankles or sagging body.

Not yet.

I was a young and sprightly 42. I walked 6 km a day, pushing that double pram. I swam. I chased two-year-old twins in the park, up and down the oval, around the swings, over the monkey bars. I had energy to burn. Until 8:00 every night, when I put Alex and Adelaide to bed and crashed. But I couldn't really remember the last time I slept through the night, so the energy I had to burn was spent.

Gary with the square glasses and the friendly face, and his off-sider Craig, pushed me into the ED. I clung onto my backpack and hoped they would hurry up and send me home. Gary could tell the nerves were starting to settle in. 'They'll do a blood test. Something like this happened to a friend of mine and it got better pretty quickly.' Looking back, I think he was trying to reassure me, but my foot still felt heavy. It was getting worse. It was in my ankle now. And my leg, just past my knee. And it wasn't just heavy like I'd been sitting on it, it was dead. I couldn't actually lift it up any more, not even if I concentrated and said, 'Come on foot, move. Lift.' It just wouldn't move any more. No amount of telling that foot what to do worked. To move that left leg, I had to pull the hem of my jeans. That was the only way.

It was getting harder not to think STROKE. AAA Jim's Lexicon Quarter Strength walls were a perfect canvas on which to scribble the word. There weren't many other options that came to mind apart from STROKE, and it scared the life out of me. I was too young, too strong, and my mind was too lively. But my foot wasn't, and the deadness was creeping up my leg. The deadness creeping like a living thing, taking over my body.

I didn't get one of those sunny cubicles. Craig and his not-so-friendly off-sider parked me in a hallway. I got to see all the newbies coming and going in their ambulances. A very efficient young lady doctor came and looked at me. I mean, she actually just looked at me, she didn't touch me or ask me any questions. She whispered secretively to Craig and his mate and they whispered back, all with their eyes to the ground. They didn't even look up and make the most of the walls and the curtains. Just very careful, very silent whispers. Then Dr Blonde Hair aimed her big black-rimmed glasses in my direction and yelled, 'Emergency MRI over here!'

'Did you say emergency?'

'Yes,' and she was gone with a flick of her blondness. I never saw her again.

Under the blonde instructions, Craig stood on one side of the ambulance trolley, his mate on the other. 'Three. Two. One.' And before I knew it, I was on one of those wider hospital beds. Someone must've asked me if I had allergies because I had a red hospital name tag on. Allergies to penicillin, band-aids and cats. How ridiculous. Did they really need to know I was allergic to cats? In a hospital?

My wide hospital bed started moving. Craig and his friend were gone, and I was whisked through the bowels of Royal North Shore Hospital, somewhere I'd never been before.

'This must be what it's like to be seasick,' I thought as I was raced along, my head only slightly propped up on a pillow. I looked up, behind my head, and I saw up the ample nose of the man who was pushing me. The nose led the way.

The green exit signs zoomed above me.

The wide doors went left,

then right,

then left again.

Exit signs.

Beeping call signs.

And that unmistakable smell of hospital antiseptic stung my eyes to the point of burning.

Other than 'Emergency MRI' I didn't know what was going on. MRI was a new thing to me. I had never had the experience before. I didn't know what was happening with my leg. I didn't know what was happening with the doctors. I had no idea what was going on. And I didn't like being out of control.

'Push my hand as hard as you can,' one of the doctors said to me as a hand was put against the sole of my left foot. My mind pushed but my foot did nothing. My mind kept pushing through gritted teeth. Still nothing. The face at the other end of the hand didn't flinch. 'Ok, now pull your toes against my hand. That's it,' as if I was actually doing it, 'pull towards you.' Again, my mind pulled but I could see nothing was happening.

'Tell me when you feel my pen.' I saw the pen flick off the top of my foot. I saw it. I felt nothing.

By now, my whole left leg was numb, right up to the hip. I had one leg left, but now the right toes were starting to go. They were going wherever the left leg had gone. Over the top of the rollercoaster.

MRI

Eventually, the orderly pulled me to a stop. He parked me in a tight spot and whispered to someone behind a little window. I decided I didn't like the whispering. Mum always told us it was rude to whisper in front of other people and not include them in the conversation. She was right. What were they saying? I knew they were talking about me, so why not talk to me? It wasn't like I couldn't understand them. In fact, the secret whispering made the whole situation seem worse. Not only was half my body being eaten by a mysterious paralysis, but none of the experts could tell me what was going on or how to fix it. And all I wanted was to get home to my babies.

'My name is Fiona.' Friendly Fiona didn't even say hello; she just launched straight into her spiel. 'I'll be doing your MRI today,' like I was there for an MRI every day. The rest of what Fiona said was a blur. Her voice was pleasant, soft, calm. But that rubbed me the wrong way because it was the complete opposite to how I felt. I was feeling rushed, heavy, confused. I needed them to hurry up.

Anyone who has had an MRI knows you can't wear any metal in the machine. At this stage, I was still fully dressed: black medium-heeled boots, socks, navy blue denim bootleg jeans that I really liked because they made my legs look longer, a black skivvy, and a dark brown fine wool jumper. Of course, I was also wearing knickers and a bra, and because I was a new mum who had been breastfeeding until only twelve months prior, they were certainly far from fancy knickers and bra. They were practical and comfortable, roughed about from the washing machine and dryer. Perhaps I should've taken more notice of the old wives' tale, 'never leave home without putting your good knickers on in case you get hit by a bus!' Well, hold that thought, we'll come back to getting hit by the bus later. I was also wearing my watch, earrings, and wedding and engagement rings. That was about the sum total of the jewellery I ever wore.

Fiona gave me one of those awful gowns they give you in hospitals that fits no one. The gown that is straight up and down at the front with no darts and supposedly ties shut at the back, but really just flaps open and shut, exposing your fair, bare bottom for all the world to see. Getting changed was not an easy task given that I was pretty much glued to the bed by this stage with two useless legs, both from the waist down. I could get off the bed with help, but my left leg was a dead weight that I had to lug behind me like a tree stump. There was no feeling in it all the way up to the hip by now, and no amount of telling it to move would make it do anything. It had to be physically dragged. Putting weight on it just meant it buckled underneath me like a rubber band. The right leg still worked, but it was getting tired, and I could tell it didn't like having to do all the work. The right foot had gone, and it was creeping up past the ankle. Whatever 'it' was. Neither of my legs were ever the greatest athletes, so I suppose when one had to do everything, there was an unfair distribution of effort. Why should one have to do all the work?

I was never good at accepting anyone's help. I was even worse at asking for it. Not even in this situation. The answer came out automatically: 'Would you like a hand?'

'No thanks.' Instead, I stupidly hobbled to the little change cubicle on my own, hanging on to tables and walls along the way. Changing into the bare-bottom gown could've happened so much faster if I had just said, 'Yes please. Some help would be great. I'd really appreciate that.' But no, I had to say, 'No thanks. I'm ok.' Some of us take a long time to learn.

I finally got my gown on, leaning on the wall and wrestling with the ties to make sure my modesty was protected. Fiona walked me into the humming engine room like a middle-aged lover on a first date. She took my arm and guided me across the floor, kind of pulling me towards her. I didn't realise when I said, 'No thanks, I'm ok,' how much easier it would be to actually lean on someone. If I could have even accepted such a small offer of support as holding onto someone's arm. And Fiona was someone I didn't know, so this was purely a physical support, there was no transfer of emotional support or love or anything like that. I am sure the rate of improvement for people who become ill must be so much higher when they have loving supports around them than if they are lonely or alone. There are probably studies already done on that.

'Let's undo these tabs,' Fiona said as she sat me on the table and I went to grab them. 'So they don't hurt when you're lying on them.'

'Can you see anything?' I kept my hands there, trying to protect my modesty.

Fiona moved my hands. 'You're ok.' That didn't really answer my question. 'Don't worry. We do this all the time.'

'But I don't. This is totally foreign to me.' None of what was going on was normal to me or happened all the time.

The MRI was like being squeezed into a tube that was barely big enough. By this stage, I had no idea what my left leg was doing. Or half my right leg. And there was still no indication of what was wrong. My head had a helmet over it to keep it in place, so it felt like the lid of the tube was put on, tighter and tighter. I had no idea what was coming.

'We're going to put a pillow under your legs so you're comfortable.' It was a kind thought from the young technician, but by this stage I couldn't lift my legs to help them, and it really didn't matter to me whether they used a pillow or a pile of bricks. My lower body was dead to me. There was nothing. Comfort wasn't really something that was an issue.

'We're going to leave the room now,' they told me. I was in that cavern all alone. The echoing nothingness with the strange sound of wind. It was cold, so I was pleased to have that hospital-issued waffle-weave blanket over me. I was tucked in like an ancient mummy, my arms dead straight.

My head wasn't moving in my helmet. But my eyes wandered and I clenched my chin. Someone thought it was a good idea to blu-tack laminated pictures of rivers and waterfalls around the room. I think they were supposed to help patients feel relaxed or something. It really didn't work. They just looked out of place. The room was too big. The pictures too small. There was a beeping that came every now and again. What was that?

Those ridiculous pictures started to make me angry in that room with the big glowing circle that looked like a portal to another place, like the one from that TV show Star Trek—but not the original Star Trek from the 70s, the newer version. I wondered if I would go through to another world and this nightmare would all be over. Maybe they could send me through the glowing blue ring and straight home. But then, if I went through the circle, would I end up at home with legs that worked—or these useless ones? That wouldn't be any good.

The tray I was lying on moved. The flat part of the rollercoaster. It slid me into the glowing portal, not to another world, just to another space. The MRI.

'Can you see me?' came Fiona's voice, this time from outside the room. There was a sliver of a mirror above my head. It was angled towards the outside. If I squinted through the tears that threatened to fall, I could just make out Fiona in her little box.

'Yes.' There were foam plugs in my ears, headphones over them, and then the lid of the tube. Her voice was muffled. But I could hear her, and I was glad she was there.

'We're going to start now. You'll hear some banging.' I expected it to be muffled too because of my heavily insulated ears. Boy, was I wrong!

Oh, the banging! It was as though my tube was buried in concrete and someone was jackhammering to get me out. The banging pummelled me in short bursts, and the tears welled up further:

BANG BANG BANG BANG BANG — staccato.

Burning salt stinging the back of my throat.

'Three minutes this time,' came the nurse's voice. It was so quiet I wondered if I actually heard it.

BANG BANG BAAAANG — a different pattern of hellish noise this time.

Trails of salty sweat running down my face and into my ears.

'Five minutes this time.'

More banging. More burning. More stinging.

It was relentless.

'Try to keep still. If you move, we'll have to start again.'

I didn't realise they could see me swallowing to keep the tears in my throat, or blinking to rid my eyes of the water that blinded me. Maybe I should just think about those ridiculous waterfall pictures? Compare them to the waterfall of sweat and salt running down my face.

The trolley started to wheel out. Someone came in and tied a tether around my arm. They tried to give me a needle. I shook and cried. There wasn't a vein, so they tried the other arm. Then back to the first, but this time into the back of the hand. I had to stop crying. It finally went in. It didn't taste like the methylated spirits of the CT scan. Instead, it was like cold water running through my veins. Someone replaced my blood with ice and I felt it spread from behind my hand, up my arm, down my spine, into the back of my head and through to the other side of my body. Like spider webs. It made me shiver. I didn't feel it go into my legs. There was no feeling in them.

They wheeled me back through the glowing portal and the banging and crying and clenching started all over again.

Finally, through the microphone: 'We're nearly finished.'

Thank goodness. The thought of getting out of there was almost too much. When the door to the outside world opened, the air changed. There was a swoosh that was such a relief! I was wheeled out on my tray and my helmet was released. The tears and sweat drained away, running down the side of my face and into my ear canal. I shook myself like a dog after a bath it was forced to have.

Needles

I hate needles. Always have. I got a bit more used to them when we were getting ready to have a family. We were older when we got married: I was 34 and Mike was 40. We were both very independent in our lives and our careers. I loved my job so much I really didn't think I wanted to leave it to have children. What if I didn't make a good mum? What if someone else did my job better than I did? I never became a ballerina. At this stage, I was an Assistant Principal in a wonderful school I had helped establish.

Mike was keener to have children than I was. We sort of tried, but not really. Not until 40 loomed closer for me and I really started to think I'd better do something or it would be too late.

Nothing happened, so I went along to the doctor just to check that everything was as it should be. My GP sent both Mike and I to Dr Frank Quinn at IVF Australia. I knew I was perfectly healthy, so I had nothing to worry about. Plus, I am one of eight children, so I knew I was from good breeding stock! Mike, on the other hand, had had a few brushes with death: anaphylaxis, electrocution, just the run-of-the-mill things. Plus, he wasn't as fit as me and he was now 45. In the time between having the blood tests and getting the results, I thought hard about how I would help Mike cope with hearing them—dealing with the fact that perhaps he wouldn't be able to have children and that the issue might lie with his body. In other words, how would I help him cope with the idea that he wasn't perfect?

I had a wonderful opportunity at work when my Principal took a few weeks' leave. I was able to be the Acting Principal. I was so excited, so proud, and so nervous all at the same time. I would never have dreamed I would ever have such a chance. Imagine, me: a Principal!

Things were going really well: children, parents, and staff were all happy and calm. School Photo Day came around. I was wearing a red and white dress with a red bolero. I felt great. I was happy. Confident.

The follow-up appointment with Dr Quinn, medicine man, was after school at St Leonards. After that - at night - I was going to meet Leanne, our real Principal, and our staff at Pennant Hills Golf Course for a dinner, speech night, and presentation run by the Australian Council of Educators. It was a busy afternoon. And my mind kept rehearsing how to tell Mike that the results said he couldn't have children, but that was ok. We were a team, and whatever happened to one of us happened to both of us. I knew what I was going to say to help him feel ok. I knew there were things we could do to work through it. Always as a team.

The offices at IVF Australia were always very quiet. Always adults. Dr Quinn was an easy man to be around—alarmingly handsome with his salt-and-pepper hair and his gentle voice. I sat opposite him, his desk between us, ready to ask if there was counselling for Mike. 'The results came back.' I knew it. I just hoped he would be ok.

'You have a 3% chance of falling pregnant.'

'Sorry. Could you repeat that, please? Don't you mean Mike?'

'3% chance.'

'Who?'

'You.'

I started to sweat. My hairline began to prickle and the edges of my sight went black around me, like a tunnel closing in. There was pounding in my ears and a big lump at the back of my throat. I felt ridiculous in my red.

I hadn't prepared myself for that. I knew how I was going to help Mike when I had to tell him his body was the reason we were not able to have children, but I hadn't even considered it would be me I would have to help. Dr Quinn must have told me a lot of information because I came away with armfuls of pamphlets about procedures, statistics, and chances of falling pregnant. All I could think was, I can't. It's my fault.

Over and over in my mind, I remembered what Mike had said in our marriage preparation course: 'I knew I loved you when I knew I wanted you to be the mother of my children.'

What good was I now? Three per cent?

I drove to the Golf Club where we were having the meeting. I walked into lots of chatter and catching up with people we recognised from other schools. I couldn't say anything to anyone. I had to pretend all was fine in my red dress and bolero. I felt like a fool, all trussed up, when all I wanted was to go home and hide.

Then dinner. Three courses. It seemed to go on for ages. I have no idea what we had. I don't even know if I ate. Then there were two speakers: one spoke about boys' education and one from the Butterfly Foundation spoke mainly about girls. It was hard enough listening to the talk about the boys, but the Butterfly lady spoke about how we just have to - above all else - love our children. I kept thinking, *Three per cent. I basically can't have any.* I had to stare straight ahead and not move my head because I would have cried. I don't know how I didn't. The tears were there; I just didn't let them roll.

The night got harder. After the speakers, representatives from the Australian Council of Educators presented awards to people. Most of them knew they were being awarded, but then they said, 'Now this person is not aware they are getting an award. This award is for building community spirit and for establishing and conducting the school Verse Speaking Choir. It is awarded to Mary Anne Allen.' Then tears came. I had to stand very still. I couldn't look at anyone I knew. Leanne knew there was something wrong. When I told her a while later about our IVF journey, she asked me if it was that day that I found out. She knew.

Our IVF journey began with the news that Mike had no problems. I had a 3% chance of falling pregnant naturally. It's funny that I was ready to help Mike accept his body if he was the one who was going to struggle to have children, but I couldn't accept myself. The process of self-injecting meant I had to get a little bit used to needles. It didn't mean I had to like them. But they were a means to an end. An awful means to a beautiful end. As a result, I went through a tricky time to get my beautiful children.

That day with my dead left leg and dying right leg, I had to have a blood test. Of course, I had to have a blood test. Always a blood test.

Then came the CT scan. This was a new experience. I had never had one before. When I tasted the methylated spirits running down my throat, I thought I was dying. I thought it was poisoning my insides. 'Don't worry. That's normal,' they told me. Normal? What was normal about losing the lower half of my body? I wanted to scream,

'There is nothing normal about this whole thing! Just get me home!'

Then there was the lumbar puncture. What can I say about that? Just before Adelaide and Alex were born, a poor unsuspecting woman who was looking forward to giving birth to her first child was injected with antiseptic during an epidural instead of anaesthetic. The poor woman was left a quadriplegic. She couldn't even cuddle her baby. I was so frightened of our epidural because I was frightened of losing control of my legs (how ironic) and worried about the mistakes that could happen.

The thought of a lumbar puncture terrified me. After all, the name says it all.

A puncture—a hole!

In the lumbar area—the spine of all places.

The idea of the Lumbar Puncture, sometimes called a Spinal Tap, was to collect the cerebrospinal fluid for diagnosis. It's a test for issues with the Central Nervous System, including the spinal cord and brain. I still didn't know what was wrong with me. I just knew Alex and Adelaide would have been awake for a few hours by now. Mum and Dad were at home looking after them, Mike was still at work, and I was doing what I was told by people who were still trying to figure out how to stop this rollercoaster.

The male nurse (or perhaps he was a doctor, I don't think I ever knew) told me I would need to bend over as far as possible to open up the gaps between the vertebrae. 'Now, make sure you keep as still as you can, because the gaps aren't very big.' And I'm not sure if they said this to me or if I just said this myself, but they were going to come at the tiny gap between the vertebrae in my spine, while I was bent over, hunched as far as I could, keeping as still as I could even though my lower back was starting to go numb. I couldn't quite tell, but I thought maybe I needed to go to the toilet. I worried I might wet myself, though I wasn't sure. After all, I hadn't been since I called the ambulance at about 1:00. And all of this was happening while I was half-exposed in one of those horrid hospital gowns that never tie up properly.

I saw the needle. It was massive—the biggest needle I had ever seen. It was about 10 cm long, just the needle part. And that was going to come at me and suck the juices right out of my spinal cord. So many things could go wrong: I might move, the doctor's hand could shake, one of us might sneeze, or the gaps between my vertebrae might be especially small from years of wearing high heels on the playground at work (a risk I made up on the spot). The needle could scrape my spinal cord; maybe my spinal cord was chunkier than expected and the needle would go right through; maybe I had too much flesh and they'd need a longer needle; maybe I'd lose balance, fall off the bed and hit my head? Could I think of any more? All of this flashed through my mind in an instant.

Well, that sounded like a safe procedure. Not.

That's when Mike arrived—about 6:00. Just as I was curled over, ready for my spinal juices to be sucked out. 'I thought you had a heavy foot?'

'I did. A few hours ago. When I called from the ambulance.'

But now it was two heavy feet, two dead legs, and a questionable bladder.

Then I met Dr Herkes.

Meet The Prof

'Hmm. Now you're an interesting case, aren't you?'

'I don't know. I don't want to be interesting. I just want to go home.'

'Well, I was on my way home and I saw your file. It's not a stroke.'

I was relieved. It had been seven hours since my foot needed instructions to move. Seven long hours of my lower half giving up on me. And the whole time, stroke was still swimming around my head. It was the worst thing I could imagine. 'That's good news.' I thought 'I'll be going home.'

'It's not meningitis.'

'That's good.' Mike was pleased about that. He seemed to understand better than I did what that meant.

'It's not a few other nasties.' Dr Herkes didn't elaborate, so I never found out what those 'nasties' were, but I can imagine they weren't pleasant. 'They've diagnosed you with Guillain-Barré.'

Blank stare from me.

'I think they're wrong. I think you have something called Transverse Myelitis.'

My blank stare didn't change. I was still grateful it wasn't a stroke (lower case now), and still hunched over from the lumbar puncture.

'All your test results have come back negative but I'm sure that's what we're dealing with.' I had no idea what this thing, this Transverse Myelitis, was. I had no idea who this Prof Herkes was either. He seemed important, he had a trail of people in white coats with clipboards and glasses following him. There must have been at least eight of them, which felt like a lot in my tiny cubicle as I recovered from having spinal fluid drained.

'If I am right I need to treat you straight away. Do I have your permission?'

All I knew was that I needed to get home, and if this Prof Herkes knew a way, I was going to take it.

'I just need to get home.'

'Right then. We'll start straight away.'

So another needle. This time with stuff going in instead of stuff coming out. Massive doses of steroids dripping into me, hopefully to stop the deadening of my body.

People think hospitals are quiet places. They are not. Alarms beep and doors swoosh, drips drip and people yell for help constantly. They are anything but quiet.

People think hospitals are peaceful places. They are not. Fluorescent lights are harshly bright and buzz most of the time. No natural light comes in. The only way patients know the difference between day and night is when the lights go from radioactive bright to deathly dark. There is no in-between. They are bewildering places.

People think hospitals are healthy places. Not necessarily. People cough and sneeze and sit in their illness. Sometimes patients choose to remain trapped in the feeling of being institutionalised. It's understandable, it feels safe that way. But it's a sad choice. It certainly isn't healthy. Yet it would be the easy way.

After the MRI and CT were cleared and showed nothing technically wrong with me, we waited for the blood test and lumbar puncture results. In the meantime, we went with Prof Herkes' gut, assuming I had this thing called Transverse Myelitis. 'When will I go home?' was all I wanted to know. I thought that since Prof Herkes now believed he knew what was wrong, he'd know how to fix me and I'd be going home. Maybe not that night, it was already late, but I thought it would be fairly soon.

One should never make assumptions.

'We will make you comfortable.'

That was what I was told.

'We will make you comfortable.'

It was said with finality.

'We will make you comfortable.'

The same answer from everyone I asked.

'We will make you comfortable.'

I wasn't going home.

Ever.

With a pat on the head, I was moved to a new home.

Ward 7F.

Ward 7F is not really a place you want to call home. It's for neurology patients. At Royal North Shore, there are 30 beds on Ward 7F, but eight of them are reserved for acute stroke patients. That was my new home from about 8.30 that night.

I was one of those eight beds.

The corner of the room was next to a window. But the view outside was just a very close, dirty-looking brick wall. Nothing else. Only grimy bricks, filthy cobwebs marking time like the patients marking time inside. I was hooked up to the drip that kept me company, and the nurses, faces blurred to me, kept telling me to try to sleep.

'We'll make you comfortable.'

It had been a long day. I closed my eyes. I didn't have a choice; my eyelids had a mind of their own. A terrible, lead-lined fog enveloped me. Like nothing I'd ever experienced. I fought so hard to stay awake, but even if I'd propped my eyelids open with sticks, they wouldn't have stayed. There was no winning against the exhaustion.

The world went black, from the edges in. My eyes went to sleep, my ears went to sleep. My legs and torso, left arm and chest were growing heavy. Not asleep, they were dead.

Until the blackness wore off.

I woke up. Opened my eyes. Tested my body: had I been dreaming? I could not move my left leg. Could not move my right leg. I smelt like a urinal; I was lying in a puddle of wee. And now I could not move my left arm. The whole left side of my torso was dead. There were long strands of hair across my pillow. And, oh no, shame of shames, I was going to wet myself again.

The fear was massive. What if every time I closed my eyes, I opened them again and more of me was dead to the world? What if I closed my eyes and it reached the point that when I opened them again, all that was left was a pair of eyes? What if I closed my eyes and the creeping deadness took over and that was it, I was gone? No one would know if I was alive or dead. I would just be two eyes in a body that wouldn't work. Two living eyes in a dead body. I just couldn't close my eyes. I just had to stay awake. I just had to fight that terrible tiredness that cocooned me. I didn't know where it came from.

Looking around Ward 7F I could only see two of my inmates and hear one of the others. I knew there were eight of us, but I was only aware of four. The other four were invisible, even to me, and I usually notice things. Little old Mrs Next to Me never physically left her bed, but mentally she was somewhere else, back in time, getting her young children ready for an outing. 'Come on dear, put your shoes on. We have to hurry. It's time to go. Do you need to go to the toilet before we leave?' No one answered her. So she turned to the next actor in her drama, 'Would you like a cup of tea, dear?' That player didn't answer either. She must have thought they hadn't heard her. 'I said, do you want a cuppa dear?'

You could tell she was getting frustrated, poor old thing. So from my bed with its view of bricks and cobwebs, I yelled into the night, 'No thanks, we have to leave, remember.'

'That's right. Get your shoes on.' And that was all she needed.

Until the next time. 'Would you like a cuppa, dear?' Little old Mrs Next to Me was on a loop.

The poor fellow opposite me and two beds down was propped so high he almost looked like he was standing. From my distance and angle, he seemed to be wearing a white helmet and a space training suit. Maybe he was, maybe he wasn't, maybe it was just my mind playing tricks and his head was swathed in bandages with a tonne of padding underneath, but it certainly wasn't the usual size of a person's head. Poor Mr Helmet. You couldn't tell how old he was or what size he was, but I decided he must have been old. Except for me, they were all old. At meal times, someone came to feed everyone in Ward 7F. Mr Helmet's goop was shovelled into his mouth, most of it sliding down his chin, along his neck and onto the hospital-issued bib, like the one at the dentist. At the end of his meal, as much could be scraped from his bib as had gone into his bowl, only now mixed with spit and the snot that ran from his nose. His swollen lips pushed most of it out of his mouth.

The nurse didn't notice, she was too busy checking beeping drips, answering invitations to tea, and stopping wannabe runaways to see that Mr Helmet couldn't eat.

The wannabe escapee was in the bed opposite me. He must have had a window view like mine. No wonder he wanted to escape. He was tall and lean, a runaway machine! At 90 years old, probably the freest of the lot of us in 7F. He would get up and walk around. I'm not sure if he was allowed to, actually, I'm not sure there even were rules in 7F. But Mr 90 didn't care. He was free and easy. Up and down, in and out of bed, from window to door. He took his toothpaste and razor to the bathroom and returned two, three, four times a day. He was on a mission to maintain dignity and cleanliness at all costs, determined to use the bathroom and toilet by himself. None of the rest of us inmates could, so he would do it for us. No sooner was he back in bed than he'd be up again, armed with some other item of self-grooming from his endless bag of tricks. And a pasty bottom bared for all the world to see as his hospital gown flapped open, revealing the whitest skin that had never seen the light of day. Mr 90 would probably have been horrified to know he was sharing bits of himself with 7F that were meant for private use. Or maybe he just didn't care.

As I looked and listened around 7F, the calling, slurping, slipping, and baring, I felt so sorry for these people. For every one of them, and their loss of dignity.

Then I realised, wait, *they think I'm one of these people.*

I *am* one of these people.

It was there, beside my viewless window, staring at the bricks through a film of not-allowed-to-fall tears and listening to the commotion behind me, that I decided I was going to write this book. I had always known I wanted to write a book, but I thought it would be a children's book or maybe a young adult one. But it was during this time that I realised I needed to write about what happened to me. To my family.

There were other people like me, my inmate buddies from 7F. Little old Mrs Next to Me, trapped in her imaginary loop; Mr Helmet with his goopy meals; and the lean, mean Mr 90 machine. They couldn't speak out about what it was like to be in that world of the Acute Stroke Ward. To be riding that rollercoaster. They couldn't say what it was like to lie under those humming fluorescent lights all day and night. They couldn't describe what it was like to have things done to them, to lose the dignity of not doing things for themselves. Plain and simple, they could not speak.

But I could.

I still can.

Thank goodness I did not lose that power. Because to speak and to have a voice is a power. Even if you can't do anything else, if you have a voice, you have a strength. A power. A superpower. Thank goodness I didn't lose that. Looking around 7F, I realised that.

I will never take it for granted.

When I was in Year 10, I had a wonderful English teacher, Mrs Purdy. She was incredibly glamorous with her straight blonde bob and her tiny frame. She had amazing ideas, spoke them quickly, and filled the blackboard with her thoughts. I loved English. That and History were my favourite subjects. I just loved to learn. I used to get in trouble in Maths for asking, 'Why does that work? Why do we do it like that? How does that work?'

'Don't ask why,' I was constantly told, 'just do it.'

Until Year 11, when Mr Andrew said, 'This is what you do and this is why you do it.' Mr Andrew looked like that TV character from the '80s, *The Greatest American Hero*. He was a hero to me because he explained everything. He transformed me from a Maths hater to a Maths lover. I ended up winning a trophy for coming first in Maths in both Year 11 and Year 12.

Mrs Purdy challenged us with poetry and books, with reading and writing. We read *To Kill a Mockingbird*. Coupled with Mrs Purdy's quick mind, Atticus Finch particularly inspired my 16-year-old self. He was like my Dad, quiet and wise, with a beautiful Christian way about him. Mrs Purdy picked a scene from the book. I wish I could remember which one. 'Write about this scene. But do it from the perspective of Boo Radley,' she said.

So I did.

I got into Boo's head and pushed and poked around. I got to know his family and his situation. I felt what life was like walking in someone else's shoes. That's always so important, to think about life from another's perspective. I used his language, Scout's language, and Atticus Finch's language. I loved rummaging around in their minds. When I got the assignment back, scrawled across the top in great big angular red letters, Mrs Purdy had written, *'Move over, Harper Lee!'*

It was thrilling! I will never forget that thrill. I closed the book before anyone saw it. My hair itched from the heat of excitement. I tried not to look around because I had to hide my thrill from everyone. I didn't want anyone to know that amongst all the Stings and George Michaels, Michael Jacksons and Madonnas, I wanted to be a Harper Lee!

Before that, I knew I enjoyed writing. My nightly journal was my best friend, my way of processing the world. But it was at that point that I was given the gift of confidence, to know that maybe I was pretty good at it. That it didn't have to be just for me.

That maybe I could use it as a voice.

I don't want to take it for granted.

Going for a Walk

My eyelids worked so hard to stay open. The lights were so bright in that acute ward of 7F, but they didn't help me stay awake. My body kept fighting my brain's attempt to sleep. It was so hard to stay conscious. And I had to stay awake for fear of dying. That's how it feels when I look back now, although at the time I didn't admit it, I just knew I was terrified parts of me would disappear. I had visions of being a floating head with only eyeballs. With no way of telling people I was still there. Really, I was frightened I would die in my sleep and that by staying awake, somehow I had control over death and could stay alive, more than just eyes in a floating head.

Mum and Dad knew I was in hospital, of course. They were with me when it all started. Thank goodness they were. If they hadn't been, if it hadn't been one of our Absolutely Ordinary Mondays, I probably would have waited to do anything about my dead leg until Mike got home from work, and by then it might have been too late. The numbness would have travelled up my leg, up my spine and Prof. Herkes would have gone home for the night. There would have been no one to call me 'an interesting case' and I could have been misdiagnosed, or just left until the following day. The lesions would have continued to travel up my spine.

'I don't know where I would be without you,' I said to Prof Herkes many years later.

'You wouldn't be.'

I knew that. Hearing it out loud was confronting. I owe Prof Herkes my life.

I told Leanne, my principal from work, and she told Kathleen, Lynette and Carmen, friends I used to work with but who were no longer there. I told my closest friends, Sandra, Christine and Gayle. That was it. Mum and Dad let my brothers and sisters know and they asked their parish to pray for me. I didn't tell anyone else at that time.

I was embarrassed. I was ashamed that my body had given up on me. That is a terrible feeling. What did I have to be ashamed of? It was as if I had done something wrong. What had I done wrong? Absolutely nothing. It's not like I chose to give up and stop moving, far from it.

Mike told some people. I know he did because we lived next door to his best friend. 'You can't imagine what it's like for Mike to live with a disabled wife,' I was told when I finally got home. With my one working arm I waved my body up and down and said in a voice that let the kindly neighbour know how outraged I was, 'This ... this is the disabled wife.'

Leanne told her sister Alison, who was in charge of the Emergency Department at Royal North Shore at the time. It must have been the second night I was a 7F resident that Alison came to visit. She arrived armed with a wheelchair. Mike was there. Mum and Dad were at home with Alex and Adelaide. Not an Absolutely Ordinary Monday, it was a Tuesday, and far from ordinary. Alison put me in the chair, scooped me out of bed and got me into the wheelchair with absolute precision. We escaped 7F and went for a walk.

Well, technically Alison and Mike went for a walk; I went for a roll. I was dressed like Mr 90 in a backless hospital gown stamped with NSW Health. I couldn't feel whether the breeze was on my back because I couldn't feel my back at all now. I was very conscious of that, making sure I held those tabs together and didn't expose as much of me as Mr 90 exposed of himself, poor fellow. He didn't seem to care.

Alison took Mike and me in the lift to the ground floor of the hospital. I was hoping we might leave, as if I'd be magically cured as I rolled out the doors. But there was no such luck. We stayed inside. The ground floor had just been through some renovations, so she pushed me around and showed me what had been done. Alison had a jovial tone to her voice, which was kind, but it didn't quite match the situation. Here I was, paralysed, living in an acute stroke ward, while a happy conversation rattled on above me about renovations and how great the hospital looked. I didn't want to be there. I didn't want to hear it. I wanted to hear how I was going to get home.

We rolled along 'The Heritage Wall' by Robyn Stacey. There were all these amazing photographs of tools and paraphernalia used by doctors and nurses throughout the hospital's history. The photos weren't merely plastered on the wall; they were backlit. It really was impressive. One picture stood out: a model of a torso showing the insides of the human body. I don't know why that one caught me, maybe because we'd had something similar at high school, or maybe because I was wondering which part of that body was failing me.

There was also a huge mural that looked like it was made of glass. It was full of blues and reds, yellows and oranges. Lots of circles joined together by swathes of colourful rectangles. It looked Indigenous, though the palette wasn't typical. I've looked it up since, it's called 'Water, Earth, Fire, Air.' The colours are exactly right for that. It is beautiful. I remember being overwhelmed by the massive scale of the piece as I sat in the wheelchair thinking, 'I don't want to be here. I don't want to be here looking at this. I just want to go home.'

It was an eerie place to be. It must have been late because the lights weren't terribly bright and we were the only people in that gigantic, cavernous space. It felt as if we were locked in, trapped inside. It genuinely felt like I was locked in my own body. By then I couldn't even get myself to the toilet. I just had to lie in bed, wet or soil myself, then press the nurse button. And when the nurse didn't come I had to press it again and again. So yes, I was trapped.

Prof Herkes (yes, his followers called him 'Prof Herkes') came to see me on about the third day. He wanted another MRI. He said the first scan, done the day I arrived, was clear, but he wanted a follow-up. Years later, at one of our appointments, he told me he got in a lot of trouble for ordering the second scan. 'But it was clear,' the MRI department had told him, 'just three days ago. There's no point wasting funds and doing the test again.'

'Just humour me,' he'd said. He copped flak for wasting hospital resources on one patient, redoing the MRI so soon after the first. The scan on 15 July 2013 was absolutely ordinary. It had nothing to show.

On 18 July the scan came back showing Prof Herkes' gut diagnosis was right. I had transverse myelitis. There were lesions blocking my spine from T8 to C4. Had he not treated me with steroids when he did, I wouldn't be here to tell this tale, the lesions would have reached my brain. With TM the damage to your body is determined by the level of damage to the spinal cord. Damage to the Sacral nerves (five vertebrae in the pelvic area) mean decreased control of hips, legs, bladder, bowel and sexual function. Moving up the spine, injury to the Lumbar area (the next five vertebrae) results in further loss of control of hips, legs and sexual function. There are 12 vertebrae that control the trunk and some respiratory muscle function because of lost intercostal movements; and the seven cervical vertebrae control the upper limbs, C7 impacts hand dexterity, C6 limits wrist and hand control, C5 affects shoulders and biceps and usually means loss of everything below that. Damage to C4, where my lesions were halted thanks to Prof Herkes, means significant loss at the shoulders and below (Praxisinstitute.org). Injury to C1–C3 typically results in loss of neck function and diaphragm control, requiring a ventilator. I was very lucky. It was so close.

Prof Herkes looked at me with that half smile. He had a way of making you feel comfortable once you got to know him, and you didn't blame him for diagnosing us for Transverse Myelitis. His voice was calm and, despite having all those young groupies, he wasn't arrogant, quite the opposite. He would sneak away from his posse to visit me privately. He listened to the noise of my inmates, sniffed the air, looked at my view and said, 'We need to get you out of here. You're not going to get better here.'

'Yes please.'

'Somewhere with a window,' he said. 'You need a window.' And before long I left my roommates and had my own room. With a window. The difference was, this window had a view.

What Difference a View Makes

My new room, still on Ward 7F, had a window. Just as promised by Prof. Herkes. It was a great big window. A great big window with a great big view across North Sydney to the Harbour. I could see the beautiful bright lights of the city and the clear night sky. I could see the big red sign that said ACU, Australian Catholic University. The coloured lights twinkled and sprinkled the dark.

When I was little, Mum and Dad used to take my brothers, sisters and me for drives during the day and night around the Hawkesbury. One of the favourites was going to look at the fairy lights at night. They started doing this when I was a baby because I was a bit of a devilish sleeper. As a baby, I would be awake for two hours, asleep for twenty minutes, and then awake for another two hours. Poor things must have been exhausted.

They worked out that they could get me to sleep in the car. And so began the tradition for our whole family of visiting Fairy Land. We went so often. Fairy Land was actually the RAAF (Royal Australian Air Force) base at Richmond. We used to say they were fairy lights because the little landing lights twinkled in the dark. There were lights of red and green and white. Of course, they all meant something to the pilots and RAAF staff, but we didn't know that. To us, they twinkled and belonged to the fairies, the pixies and the goblins.

When it rained, the lights refracted on the water drops on the car windows in the dark. The fairies couldn't come out on wet nights. Everyone knew that fairies couldn't let their wings get wet. Fairies with wet wings couldn't fly. It was very dangerous for them. On clear nights, we imagined fairies and elves fluttering and flying in and out of the hangars, which of course were their homes. There was a whole little world out there that was open to the imagination. It was extra special when the landing lights were on. They swooshed along the runway at high speed. The signs along the road warned drivers not to be distracted, but it was impossible not to stare at them and be captivated, they were so hypnotic! They carried you along from one end of Fairy Land to the other at warp speed.

I've always loved the look of lights at night, the way they dance and pop.

My window view from 7F brought peace because it was a veritable Fairy Land. I could imagine flying above it with Peter Pan and Wendy. Soaring between the buildings, I didn't need my legs to work. I could just float on the breeze. Seeing the big red ACU sign was comforting because I had done all my study at ACU (not at North Sydney) and I had been doing some marking work for the Australian Catholic University. I knew people there, I knew I was needed, and there were people who cared about me. I knew that I was respected there. I knew that it was a special place. Most importantly, I knew that Mary Mackillop Place was right there under that building.

I have always drawn great strength from Mary Mackillop. The day that Mary was canonised, 17 October 2010, was a wonderful, celebrated day.

Australia's first saint.

A woman.

A teacher.

A daughter.

A sister.

A person who worked to allow access to education for all, regardless of their economic or social standing.

Someone who spoke up for what she believed, to the point of being excommunicated from the Catholic Church.

A voice for the voiceless.

Mary was everything that I would strive to be.

The school where I worked, Holy Cross, celebrated Mary's canonisation beautifully and with great love. Each grade, from Kindergarten to Year Six, planted a rose bush in her honour, a Mary Mackillop rose. It was specially developed for the canonisation. A lovely soft pink rose on a short shrub with a faint perfume. We shared a Mass and invited parents to join us for a picnic in the playground. There are beautiful songs about Mary Mackillop and the Australian landscape, and how she is - not was - a woman of our land:

Across these great lands she brought the Good News,

With courage and love in her heart

That faith and hope may live

Beneath a Cross of Stars, beneath a Cross of Stars

(A Cross of Stars) , Andrew Chinn, 2004

I was a frequent visitor to Mary Mackillop Place in North Sydney when we were going through IVF and when I was pregnant. I went to Mass there and wrote many lines of heartfelt prayers on little slips of paper that went into the prayer box at Mary's tomb. I sat with her for many visits; sometimes for minutes, sometimes longer, sometimes in silence, sometimes questioning, sometimes listening, sometimes asking. I felt that Mary and I knew each other well. I had her on speed dial!

Just as a side note, it didn't matter how much we tried to look after the pretty pink Mary Mackillop roses, they all went to Heaven to meet their maker and found their way to the compost bin! Dad had more success with his Mary Mackillop roses. He loved to grow them, and when they bloomed, he picked them for Mum. They kept them in the lounge room in a little old crystal vase. The perfume filled the room.

Late one night, Mum and Dad came to visit me in my new room with a view. It must have been very late because Mike wasn't getting home from work until Mum and Dad had Alex and Adelaide ready for bed. It was a coping strategy.

They came to see me in my new room in 7F. Mum brought my blue fleece jacket. I hadn't seen or spoken to my babies since I got to the hospital about a week ago, and she and Dad were getting them ready to come and see me. They were talking about lights and cords and buttons. But Mum thought it was a good idea for them to see me in clothes they were used to, not the hospital-issued gown with no back. She was right. Mum was very wise. They had been drawing pictures of Mummy and all sorts of things. Mum and Dad were getting them ready. When my friend Gayle asked me if there was anything I needed, all I could think to ask for was a hairbrush and a headband. Gosh, that made a difference!

The night that Mum and Dad came, they looked tired. They had been driving from Windsor to Lane Cove to be with Adelaide and Alex because Mike kept going to work. He didn't stop. In peak hour, that was a two-hour drive, so they were getting up early and leaving home before 6 am to beat the morning rush and get to Lane Cove before Mike left for work. They stayed until Mike got home at night and then drove home. And they weren't young. I can't tell you how grateful I still am for what they did during that time. I said to both of them that while ever I could not be there with my babies and Mum and Dad could, it felt like part of me was there. I called a nannying place to send someone, but we didn't know them. So Mum and Dad were the Absolutely Ordinary, the consistent presence for Alex and Adelaide, while I couldn't be there.

I know Mum and Dad were worried. I get worried whenever one of my babies is sick or hurt, and I was still a baby to

Mum and Dad. They would have felt the same. Their (grown-up) baby lying in a huge hospital bed, surrounded by lights and drips and the name of things we'd never heard of.

'You have to imagine that you can move,' said Mum. 'Just imagine you can move.' She was desperate. 'Even if you can't feel anything. Just imagine you can move those toes.' Mum was very wise. 'Picture those toes moving in your head.' I could feel Mum willing my body to move through her words. She was desperate for something to happen. If she could have ripped me out of that bed and carried me down the seven levels of hospital to the car park to get home, I know she would have. The desperation lines on her face as she said again, 'Just imagine,' showed how much she wished she could trade places with my limp body. If it would have made any difference, she would have jumped in that bed next to the window with the view and taken my place.

Dad just listened. He couldn't say anything. He listened to Mum repeat, 'Pretend you can feel something.' There was nothing for him to say. He listened and stared out that window. I wonder if he remembered Fairy Land as well.

I had to be upbeat for them.

'Mum, Dad. I'll be OK. Look out that window.'

We all looked out the window.

The sky was inky black.

We looked at the fairy lights.

We looked at the stars.

'See the ACU building?' Everyone took their few seconds to find it and look at it. The sign was big, bright and bold. Red against the blackness.

There was a silent 'yes' between us. 'Yes', we could see that sign, brazen in the night. A beacon.

'Mary Mackillop is buried there.'

My left big toe moved.

After the Big Toe

No one has ever celebrated a big toe as much as that big toe. Not in the history of all big toes! Three pairs of eyes stared in disbelief and fear that perhaps we had imagined what we just saw. We willed it to happen again. The movement was so minuscule that it could have been mistaken, especially in the dark. You see, this room, this private room, was dark. It wasn't like the stark light of the Acute Stroke Ward. In here, I could control how bright or dim I had the lights.

I didn't realise it until I got in here, but my head was in pain. It had been hurting the whole time. It wasn't pounding or drumming or anything like that; it was simply aching really badly. And joy of joys, when I arrived in my new room, my period arrived. I could not feel most of my body, but I could feel the pain from that.

We take so much for granted in our day-to-day lives. Having a shower, for example. Until it is taken away. It was not that I couldn't have a shower, it was that I could not have a shower alone. My independence was gone. First, I had to wait until someone could take me to the shower. Then I had to wait for the water to be adjusted. I had to wait to be put on a shower chair. I had to wait for someone to take my clothes off. They made sure I was OK in the shower space. Thankfully, they walked out while I showered, but they came back in to turn the water off, dry me, and dress me. A grown adult with no privacy. No dignity.

'Don't worry, dear,' the nurses all said the same thing. 'We do this every day.'

'But I don't.'

The only interesting thing I could talk to the nurses about, that raised spirits at this time and took attention away from life and death, was the Royal Baby. The world was in waiting. Princess Catherine and Prince William were expecting their first baby, and the world's media was camped out in front of St Mary's Hospital in London. Union Jacks were flying, and I think even Republicans were secretly following the story.

'No baby yet,' RNSH (Royal North Shore Hospital) staff announced each time they came into my room. 'Not yet.' They must have had a sign on my door. It was something that made me happy.

That could change really quickly, though. I never knew when I would need to go to the toilet. I never knew until after it was too late. I pressed that button, pressed it and pressed it. But it didn't matter how many times or how hard; I still had to sit there for what felt like forever in my filth and embarrassment.

'Don't cry. You don't need to cry. Stop that crying.' They would say as they tried to wedge a bedpan underneath me.

'There's no point,' I said through gritted teeth as the plastic bedpan stuck to the skin on my legs when the nurses tried to force it underneath my sodden, stinky bottom. 'I've already been. It's too late. I'm wet.'

I did need to cry. I don't think I cried enough. I did need to cry while someone changed my clothes and someone else showered me. I did need to cry while I watched someone strip the bed of my urine and faeces, and I listened to the plastic hospital mattress cover being washed and dried. I did need to cry when I felt the fourth new white sheet that day float through the air like a parachute to land on my bed and be tucked in with detached efficiency. And I did need to cry when I was put back into the bed, ready for the whole process to start again.

I needed to cry about a body that didn't work. About legs that couldn't hold me or move me, about legs that couldn't carry my children. I needed to cry when I realised the nurses were sick of changing my sheets and I had a little plastic bag attached to my bed, filling up with golden wee. I wanted to cry when I realised that bag tied to the bed was there for all to see what was coming from my insides. Again, I was embarrassed. It wasn't my fault, I didn't cause it, but I was embarrassed. I needed to cry.

But I didn't.

I cried about the wrong things. I didn't cry about my arm that wasn't strong enough to give the tight cuddles I used to give. I should have, but I didn't. I saved up all those tears.

'Don't cry, dear. You don't need to cry about the bed.'

I did need to cry. I didn't cry enough.

'I think my hair is falling out.' I held up a big handful of it.

'Oh no, that's normal,' the nurses told me. 'No baby yet,' and out they would run, changing the topic so they wouldn't get stuck telling me the truth about the tufts of hair.

My hair was falling out. It was coming out in great clumps. It came out in handfuls when I washed it, dark against the white hospital bathroom non-slip tiles. It was all over my pillow like a mohair shawl. It was definitely falling out. I didn't really have all that much to lose.

Then came the rash. How could I not feel my left leg, my right leg, my torso, bladder, bowel, left arm, left hand, except for the thumb and pointer finger, but I could feel period pain and that rotten rash! How was that possible? It started to drive me crazy. I was covered in it. Like one of those horrid pictures that scares the life out of you when you look up Dr Google, even though you know you shouldn't, and it shows you the absolute worst case of something like eczema, dermatitis, chicken pox, leprosy, or some other deadly thing with which you diagnose yourself after a "helpful" internet search of symptoms.

It turned out to be an allergy to the steroids that saved my life. It wasn't really a competition: rash or death? Period pain and itchy skin rash could break through anything. Who would have thought? Good to know! Period pain and skin rash can beat even the strongest paralysis. They must be industrial strength to get through what I was going through!

Some of the young doctors came to see me on about the sixth day. I didn't recognise them without their revered leader. They told me how lucky I was to have Prof Herkes, but they always said his name so fast, and I was always getting over the 'Prof' part rather than his name starting with Doctor. I thought it was a bit strange. I couldn't remember whether his name was Herkees, Herk-us, Herks, or some other derivative. It took me a long time, and it wasn't until a wise receptionist said, 'It's Herkes, as in Circus.' What an easy way to remember it! I wish they had said that at the beginning.

These young pups were too serious to tell me whether there was a young prince or princess on the other side of the world. I knew I would have to wait for the nurses for that information. These people were here to check charts and things, and probably to earn points for themselves. They still couldn't tell me when I was going home or what was happening.

Only the Prof could tell me that.

Prof Herkes came one day on his own. I hardly recognised him without the fanfare of his groupies. He was very serious. I knew he was very important.

'I don't really know what is wrong with me.'

'I told you. Don't you remember?' I felt well and truly scolded. His voice was annoyed. 'You have Transverse Myelitis.' I really did not hear the rest because from his tone, I could tell I obviously should have remembered from a previous time that I was told. Maybe I was told when Mr 90 was streaking across the room and I was distracted by the bare white bottom mooning everyone?

Hearing, or perhaps understanding, popped back into gear when the Prof started talking about rehabilitation hospitals. 'We've got your name down at this one and that one. Mt Wilga would be the preference because of their work with spinal cord injuries, but it's further away and harder to get into. We just have to wait and see. You'll be here until a place comes up and then we'll move you. Do you have any questions?'

'I don't think so.'

'We don't know what the outcome will be. You'll work with the physios and the OTs and maybe speech therapists. There will be psychologists. We don't know how long you'll be there. It can be anywhere from six weeks to six months. It just depends on the person and how things progress.'

What?

Rehab?

This was a new, low blow. I had never given Rehab a thought. I thought they would make me better and send me home in a couple of hours. Like when I was in the Emergency Department, I thought they would give me something for the heavy leg, maybe do a blood test, let me have a little rest, and send me on my way. But they had to keep me. This was six days later. And now they had to keep me again. It was like a never-ending bad dream from which I was never going to escape. Six weeks to six months? How could I be away from my children for that long? How could Mum and Dad be driving down to be with them for that long?

Then came the next piece of information from Prof Herkes. But I would have to shelve this. I could not let this piece of information in too deep. 'They say one third of people with TM get better. One third improve with residual impacts. One third are left with a permanent disability and don't improve at all.'

I was just too exhausted to let that in. I knew I would have to let that go and deal with that piece of information another time. 'I am so tired. I just can't even keep my eyes open. I'm fighting and my body just can't stay awake. My brain can't think and I just can't do anything.'

'That sounds like the medication.'

'I've never been so tired. I had Glandular Fever years ago, and Chronic Fatigue, and it's even worse than that. I just can't stay awake. I can't think and I can't move.'

'Yes. That's definitely the meds. We'll stop that.' He looked at the one doctor who was with him, nodded his head and said, 'Straight away.'

And just like that, with two simple words and a nod of the head, Prof Herkes stopped the mind-numbing medication. It was Endone: Oxycontin. He had prescribed the medication because he knew what was in store for me. He knew that the usual pathway for Transverse Myelitis was paralysis, followed by pain.

Wise man.

I certainly appreciated that he listened to me and gave me back the ability to stay awake. Dr Herkes was wonderful like that: he was a listener.

Then he added, 'But it is really important that you rest. Don't forget that. Rest is just as important as everything else. Without it, you won't recover.'

To this point in my life, I'd had four visits to hospital. One was the week before I started my very first teaching job. My perfectly straight teeth were on the move because of four enormous impacted wisdom teeth. I know they were enormous because I kept them in a specimen jar after they were taken out, for years. That's a bit disgusting really! The lower two were fused to my jaw. This visit to hospital was only an overnight stay, but I came home sore and swollen. The following week, my bruises turned the colours of the rainbow, making me look like a radioactive soccer ball, swollen and glowing. It was quite impressive.

Another visit to hospital was one I don't remember, but Mum and Dad did. They told the story with fear about a sky-high temperature that sent me into convulsions. It was the result of a particularly bad gastro virus.

The first visit I do remember happened when I was 17 months old. I had my tonsils out at Windsor Hospital. This building was originally constructed as barracks for male convicts in 1820, then acquired as a hospital in 1846. It's a beautiful building, but cold and rough by today's paediatric ward standards, by any hospital standards really. The children's ward wasn't like they are now, where parents are expected to stay and the walls are bright with happy pictures. I remember beige stone walls with a door that closed. There were glass windows so nurses could look in as they walked past, and cots with metal bars for babies like me. I don't recall any soft furnishings or other children. There was one picture of a tree stuck on the wall.

When I woke in my lonely cot, there was a clear cord stuck in my arm, with a thick bandage wrapped around my hand. It led to a strange-looking bag I'd never seen before. I stood at the bars of the cot and watched the cleaner polish the floor. He used one of those gigantic, noisy machines with the fluffy pad underneath. To my baby brain, it seemed to float above the checkerboard laminate like a hovercraft. I wondered what would happen if that spinning thing rolled over the cord. Would it whip around and suck it up like a snake? I wasn't scared; I just watched it all happen.

The next part of the memory isn't mine, it's Dad's, and he always thought it was hilarious. When the nurses came in to see me in that old hospital room, I wasn't worried about going home, like I was as a 42-year-old. Instead, I was far more concerned about the culinary offerings I'd been given: ice cream, jelly, mashed potato, pureed vegetables.

According to the nurse, I stood there, drip in arm and gripping the inside of the cot in all my baby-ness, and demanded, 'Get me some food,' then followed up with, 'and make it something sensible!'

You know, I think Dad was rather proud that he had a daughter who could stand her ground from that age and announce what she wanted. I had a voice right from the beginning. That little anecdote even made it into Dad's wedding speech.

Another stay in hospital was when they found the melanoma. What a shock that was. I was only 29. There was a small spot on the back of my thigh. First the GP said, 'Don't worry. It's only small. Because it's changed, we'll get rid of it. I'll send you to the dermatologist.'

The dermatologist said the same thing: 'Don't worry. It's only small. Because it's changed, we'll get rid of it.' So we did. 'Come back in two weeks to have the stitches out.'

Until the next day, when I had phone messages left for me at home, work and on my mobile. 'It's melanoma. You need to come back straight away.'

So the next stay in hospital was a date with a plastic surgeon who cut a massive chunk out of my thigh to save my life. I tell everyone to get their skin checked at least once every twelve months. It's so important. You just never know what could be lurking beneath the surface.

The most energising hospital stay was when I went in to have my babies. Because we were going through the IVF process, we were closely monitored. We found out very early that we were pregnant. They tell you not to do your own pregnancy test, but to wait for their blood test at, I think, eight weeks. This was our fourth cycle. We were so excited when the result came back positive. At the first ultrasound, I hoped they'd say we were expecting twins. I asked them to transfer two eggs this time. Mike asked, 'Do you think you can cope with twins?'

'Of course we will cope.'

'No. Do you think you can cope?'

'Of course I can.'

I was so thankful for the news that we were expecting twins. 'You're expecting twins at the moment,' then came the caveat, 'but come back next week and there'll probably only be one. Baby A hardly has any fluid in the sac around it. Compare that to Baby B, where you can see it floating around.' One baby was tiny, with the walls of the sac almost touching it, no black fluid. The other, by comparison, was twice the size, with the sac walls pushed far out and plenty of blackness surrounding it. Each ultrasound brought the same warning: 'At the moment there are twins, but come back next week and prepare yourself that there will only be one.'

Oh my goodness, it was awful. Before every ultrasound I had to brace myself to hear those words I'd heard in our first cycle: 'There is not a heartbeat.' What they really mean is, 'Your baby is dead.' They just can't say it.

But not this time. We were so excited with each passing week. We got to the 33rd week. 'Baby A is doing really well.'

'That's great news.'

'But Baby B is going backwards.' That rollercoaster again. 'You'll be having these babies on Monday.' That was Friday.

I raced to Target like a crazy pregnant woman. I hadn't bought any baby clothes because I didn't know how close to term we'd get, or what sizes I'd need. The smallest I could find was 00000, so I bought a range of Bonds suits in 00000 and 0000, along with singlets, socks and blankets. I didn't know what we were having, Mike did, because I wanted a surprise. It's not very often, as an adult, that there are opportunities for genuine, beautiful surprises in life, so I wanted to take that chance when I could. I filled my trolley with sensible whites and pale greens and yellows.

I felt my tummy and I just knew. I had known from the beginning that one of my babies was a girl and the other a boy. And I knew which was which. So I put a pink suit and a blue suit, a pink wrap and a blue wrap in the trolley amongst the neutrals. 'You can always take them back if you're wrong,' I told myself, hoping I wouldn't have to.

At 34 weeks, babies' lungs aren't strong enough to be born. So I drove into hospital on the Friday afternoon, Saturday and Sunday to have injections (more needles) of steroids. Each day two monitors were strapped around my belly and I could hear the beating hearts, see the numbers of beats. I was getting to know my babies before they came. I was lucky to spend so much time with them before they were even born, just the three of us.

It was dark at 5 am on 28 March 2011 when we were getting ready to go to hospital. Dark and chilly. We took one photo of me with my pregnant belly at home before we left and arrived well and truly before the expected time of 6 am. I was such a jumping jack of emotions. I wanted to giggle with excitement, but at the same time I wanted to burst apart with fear, because I really did not want that epidural. I was more worried about that than being sliced open and having two babies pulled out of me.

I wore a red hair net and wrist band because of allergies, and one of those bottom-exposing hospital gowns. The absence of darts means they're definitely not made to fit a pregnant body, let alone one carrying twins! There were so many people in that little room with me. I hardly recognised anyone until Dr MacGibbon spoke. Her mousy curls were hidden under her doctor's hat and mask, and her usual professional attire was covered by two gowns like mine, one done up at the front and the other at the back. Why didn't I get two? She had such a quiet voice, so I was shocked when I heard her order everyone to leave the room. 'There are too many people in here. It's stressing her out. We only need the anaesthetist and nurse at the moment, thank you. Everyone else I will see you in surgery.' They all marched out like little lost blue sheep. Now there were just Mike and I, Dr MacGibbon, and the two I couldn't even see. It made such a difference. I changed from a jumping jack to a half jumping jack.

It didn't take long for the epidural to work. 'I can't feel my legs.'

'Good. That means it's working.'

Not feeling my legs was very different that day. That was what was meant to happen.

'When you get home, you can decide where the pictures go on the walls.' Mike was trying to distract me. He knew how scared I was. I had organised a fellow to come and paint the house while I was in hospital, Korean John. It was supposed to take three days and Mike was supposed to be able to stay in the house while he did the work.

'What are you going on about! Don't talk to me about paintings on the wall now! Not appropriate!' I wasn't very receptive to his attempts at distraction at that particular point in time.

We wheeled into the next room. A screen was put up between my chest and lower body so I couldn't see them cut me open and reach inside. You know, I think I would have liked to watch. Mike got the option. 'Please tell me everything that's going on. I just need to know. Then I'll be ok.'

'You will feel pressure, but you shouldn't feel pain. If you feel pain, tell me.'

A baby cried. 'It's a girl!' I saw that body held up high like a trophy; all arms and legs flailing. That skinny little girl was shot through the air like a rocket, wrapped in a blanket and put on my chest. 'Oh Mike, it's a girl!' I held her tight, told her I loved her, and in that instant I knew I never wanted to let her go. And I happy cried.

Another baby cried and the girl baby was whisked away to warm up. 'It's a boy!' Another trophy with flailing legs and arms. Another rocket shot through the air, wrapped in a blanket and placed on my chest. This time a skinny little endangered boy body.

'Oh Mike, it's a boy!' I happy cried some more. I held him tight, told him I loved him, and knew I would hold him forever.

Boy baby was whisked away to warm up. 'Go with them, Mike.' I was left alone to have the hole in my body stitched back together, and to happy cry alone.

I stayed in hospital for five days. It smelled like fairy-blue Angel hand disinfectant. It has the softest scent; it doesn't burn the hairs off your nostrils when you walk past, or strip the flesh off your bones if you have to use it all the time. Whenever I see or smell the Angel brand hand wash, I'm taken right back to North Shore Private Hospital and our time there.

Alex and Adelaide stayed in hospital for four weeks. To go home without them, after carrying them inside me for nine months, was like losing part of myself. I was there every day. Sometimes Mike came before work, sometimes after. The NICU nurses were like worker bees, buzzing around day and night. They taught us how to help our babies learn to suck. They showed us how to bathe them, change them and soothe them. Those NICU nurses were incredible. For the first few years, I sent them, Dr Quinn and Dr MacGibbon, thank you letters on our birthdays. Our family was a true medical team effort, very different from the book Mum read to me, Where Do Babies Come From, all those years ago. Our babies didn't just involve a Mummy and a Daddy, but a Mummy, a Daddy and a whole lot more!

That stay in hospital gave me the most life-giving experience I've ever had.

Nothing like this time at RNSH.

I knew by now that supplies at home would be running low. So my newly awakened mind, no longer addled by the drugs Prof Herkes had ordered to be stopped, along with my right arm and my trusty mobile phone, went to work. I loved the Woolworths app. I ordered groceries for home delivery. Like my 17-month-old self, I was going to place an order, and I was going to make it something sensible! I was ordering blind, relying on memory and knowing what would be needed.

Toilet paper – always a necessity,

nappies – two-year-old girls,

nappies – two-year-old boys,

baby wipes,

garbage bags – vanilla scented, large,

Napisan Gold powder,

Omo front loader, sensitive skin,

A2 milk, 2 litres,

bread – two loaves, white sliced with hidden fibre,

fish fingers – 48 I&J,

frozen baby peas – 500 grams,

tinned corn – four small, super sweet,

eight bananas,

four navel oranges,

potatoes – red, 2 kg,

two Hass avocados,

strawberries – 2 punnets,

eggs – 12 free range,

baby food pouches – 2 x lasagne, 2 x tuna mornay, 2 x chicken casserole.

I didn't need to order a cauliflower or a cabbage because Dad said he would bring those from his brother John, who had grown them in his backyard. We didn't need tomatoes either, because Dad had a random tomato bush growing in his compost heap. They were those tiny tomatoes that even two-year-old mouths could eat whole. The kids loved them, popping them in their mouths, biting them in half, and exploding them in a mass of seeds and juice. Mum and Dad would clap and laugh, and everyone would be happy. You couldn't buy that on the Woolworths app.

I ordered those baby food pouches so they could be snacks or fillers for mashed potato while I wasn't there. Things needed to be as simple as possible for Mum and Dad. I was very conscious of how big the job was that they were doing for our family. Huge.

The Woolworths order arrived while Mum and Dad were at the house. 'No, you really don't need to put it away, but if you don't mind putting the cold stuff away, that would be great.'

The rest was left for Mike. 'You ordered doubles. You got things we didn't need,' he said over the phone. I thought I'd done well to order anything. After all, I was only just getting used to not having to fight my body and my brain to stay awake. I did that order with one arm, a head and a mobile phone. Looking back, I think I did quite well to order anything at all. At the time, I didn't argue. At the time, I didn't really have a voice. I'm only just starting to find that again now.

The Visits

Anyone who has ever been in hospital knows how important it is not to be left alone. Anyone who has ever visited someone in a nursing home would have felt the excitement in the body of their person as they get closer to give them a hello hug. First, when they hear a sound that is out of the ordinary, they look up in the hope that it might be for them, though not really expecting anything. More likely, they're looking up to see what little tidbit of news they can savour from someone else's life. Then comes that little glimpse of recognition, a flicker of unbelief, followed by youthful excitement. With Dad in the nursing home, it was almost elation, just for a visitor.

I was staring at my view one morning, just after my toe moved. I knew it was morning because I could see the traffic outside I was even wishing I could be in it. It was heading towards the Bridge for the City. I also knew because I was keeping tabs on the Royal baby, and Sunrise on Channel 7 was telling me it was about 8:30 and that nothing else was going on in the world except people queued outside that London hospital, waiting for the baby to be born. It didn't matter whether it was a girl or a boy, this would be the next in line after Prince William, since the succession laws had just been changed. This was very exciting. So I was watching my view, listening to the endless commentary on the not-yet-arrived baby, when my room went dark. Someone was in the doorway, but it wasn't a nurse, there was no cheerful, 'No baby yet!'

I turned around. There, filling the doorway, was Father George. Our Father George from Greenwich. I know I must have had that little glimpse of recognition, then a touch of unbelief, followed by youthful excitement and, like Dad, almost elation. You see, I had called the big Parish house hoping the Parish priest would come and visit, bring me the Eucharist. But no, he said he would pray for me. And here was Father George. He must have been in his 90s, and he had walked all the way from Greenwich to the hospital, two kilometres! 'Would you like the Eucharist? And a blessing?'

He gently laid his hands on my head and began to pray. I looked down.

'Through this holy anointing,' he said, rubbing the holy oil on my forehead and hands, 'May the Lord in His love and mercy help you with the grace of the Holy Spirit.' I rubbed the oil from my hands all over my face. 'May the Lord who frees you from sin, save you and raise you up.'

It would be wonderful to say that I was cured, that it was a miracle. But it was not. Neither of us expected that, of course. Father George read a Gospel passage. I wish I could remember which one, but I can't. I don't think I would have remembered even if you'd asked me straight after he finished. Maybe it was the passage about Lazarus or the paralytic.

'The Body of Christ.'

'Amen.'

Father George only came once. But he organised someone from Mary MacKillop Place to visit and bring the Eucharist. They also brought a relic of Mary MacKillop. That was very special. It always crosses my mind that when people become saints, they must somehow expand, because suddenly there are so many relics. I sometimes wonder where they all come from!

I was so sad to hear a few years later that Father George had died. I didn't know he was sick. I wish I had, because I like to think I might have been there for him as he was for me. I hope there were hundreds of people there at the end to say goodbye to Father George, I'm sure I wouldn't have been missed. That's not the point. Father George took time every week to be with Adelaide, Alex and me after Mass at the Mary Help of Christians Chapel, and he gave me such a special, private moment when he blessed me in hospital. I always thanked him, but I don't know if I ever truly let him know how grateful I was, how grateful I always will be. He was a lovely man, a gentle man. His visit meant so much, and I am so sorry I didn't get to say goodbye.

I was surprised by Craig and his partner one day when they came to visit me in 7F. I didn't expect them to remember me. Of all the people they must cart around in their ambulance each week, with serious things wrong with them, I couldn't believe they would remember a heavy foot. When I first met them, I was only a heavy foot. By the time they left me at the hospital, I was an unknown heavy leg being whisked off for an emergency MRI. In their experience, I was really only the foot. I couldn't believe they remembered me, and then, of all the people in that huge hospital, they took the trouble to find me. I surprised myself with how happy I was to see them. They trusted that I needed to be at the hospital in the first place and brought me in quickly. Thank goodness they didn't just say something like, 'Oh, you've just pinched a nerve,' or dismiss it. They trusted something was wrong and carted me in. And that day they came back to visit me. It was very emotional to realise that maybe I left an impression on them, or my leaden foot did, and they remembered who I was.

Years later, actually one year later and then again ten years on, I wrote to the NSW St John Ambulance Service and briefly told them the story of the heavy foot and of the two very kind men who believed in me and respectfully helped me. They were there at the precipice, as my family and I were about to fall, at the top of the Rolleroaster. I wonder how Ambulance paramedics remember their patients? Do they remember us as names, or faces, or just as the condition? So I wonder if they remember me as 'Mary Anne', or 'brown hair, brown eyes, freckles, lipstick'? Or was I 'leaden foot, paralysis travelling up the leg, in need of an emergency MRI, stroke and meningitis quickly ruled out'? I'm surprised they remembered me at all.

Gayle came to visit. She brought some magazines, a hairbrush and a headband. Of course, the magazines were filled, cover to cover, with predictions about the Royal Baby. The medical expert predicted a girl, the psychic predicted a boy, and the man on the side of the road dressed in a Union Jack suit with an umbrella hat said he had been there when Prince William and Prince Harry were born. They were desperate to fill those pages while waiting for the baby, the world's most anticipated news since the reveal of Princess Catherine's wedding dress designer. The magazines were a welcome relief, but to be able to drag that brush through my unkempt hair

Oh, the joy!

I can hardly describe the relief of feeling sharp, spiky bristles scratching through those thinning tresses and soothing my itching, rash-covered scalp. Hearing that sound as I dragged the spikes of that spongy mound in slow motion, eyes closed for extra effect, was like an old-fashioned wood plane scraping curls off a block of timber. Oh my goodness, I could have brushed what was left of that hair until I was bald! The feeling was euphoric, the best I had felt in ages, certainly since I had been in hospital.

And then I had a headband to keep the wayward, lonely strands in place. Like a giant elastic band. I felt half human again, only the top half. My friends from the Acute Stroke ward wouldn't have recognised me, though I don't think they would have anyway. I felt so much better. My sparse head of hair looked almost alive!

Then I put my blue fleece zip up jacket on over my bottom exposing gown. I felt almost regal!

Finally, it was time to see Alex and Adelaide. My twins. My pride and joy. Mum told me they had been asking where I was. True to form, she had told them the truth from the start.

She was so glad she hadn't made up something like so many people would, you know, 'Oh, Mummy's in the laundry,' or 'Mummy's just gone to the shop.' Because the problem with a lie like that is that I simply did not come home, and I kept not coming home. On the Absolutely Ordinary Monday, I put them down for their afternoon sleep and then called the ambulance. I thought I'd be back before they woke up. Mum told them I had to go to the hospital to be checked. She told them I was okay and the doctors were looking after me. They were only two years old. That was enough truth.

When it took longer and longer, Mum got them to draw pictures of Mummy; Mummy in bed, Mummy in bed with lights around her, Mummy in bed with lights around her holding Adelaide and Alex, and Mummy sitting in a big chair giving them a cuddle. My mum was always a good drawer. Dad, on the other hand, always drew the same person in the same pose holding a kite! They talked about saying hello and about waving goodbye at the door. Mum did a great job of preparing them. I don't know if the kite pictures helped, but Dad gave them cuddles.

Sitting in the big blue chair in the corner of my room, I was so happy to see them at that door. I can't even say I was excited, that minimises the feeling I had. I was completely overwhelmed to be able to hold my babies. A week had felt like a lifetime. They came in slowly at first, tentative.

Alex came straight to me. He didn't look around, just walked over, sat on my lap and snuggled in. The world's best snuggle. He was always such a gentle boy, a quiet, contemplative soul, even as a baby. You look at photos of him and you see wise eyes. In every photo of him as a baby and a little boy, Alex had his eyes on me. He has always taken everything in, from a safe space. I was always his safe space. Until he got older. When that changed, it cut like a knife. Worse.

Adelaide had to look around. She had to take in the lights, the smells, the sounds. 'What's this? What's in here?' She slid open a drawer, bounced open a cupboard, test drove the hairbrush she didn't recognise. She eventually made her way to Alex and me, via the bathroom, the bedside table, under the big bed and the huge window with the view. When she finally reached me, there we were: the three of us. One on each knee and me in the middle.

Together again. As we should be.

Moving Day

If I had to move, I wanted to go home. I didn't want to go from one hospital to another. And that's what they were talking about.

Rehab.

My name was down at a few different places, but I didn't know any of them. Why would I? Unless you know someone who has needed one of these places, you usually live in a world blissfully unaware of them, where they are and what they do. Life sort of runs parallel to the world of illness until you cross into it and need to join.

'Great news. There's a place at Mt Wilga,' Prof Herkes was so pleased. 'It's in Hornsby.' That's where he wanted me to go. 'Hospital transport will pick you up tomorrow. They do great work with strokes and spinal cord injuries.' I didn't really understand how that applied to me because I knew I hadn't had a stroke, and I didn't think anything had injured my spine. I still didn't really understand what had happened to my body. I couldn't get up and walk away, so I had to go along with the flow. I didn't like the flow; it wasn't easy, more like white-water rapids, but I had to go with it.

After a week and a half at Royal North Shore, it was off to Hornsby.

If Royal North Shore was forever away from my family, Hornsby was on another planet. As children, we grew up in Windsor. It was a country town in those days. Mum and Dad would always take us to North Haven, just south of Port Macquarie, for our holidays. We were lucky to have a great-aunty who lived up there. Mum's grandfather was a policeman who took his wife and three daughters up there when they were young. They cleared swamp land and built a home. He helped to build the break wall along the Camden Haven River at North Haven and shaped the community there.

We would always pack the night before we were due to leave. Mum made sure we had what she thought we would need for the time we were going, and Dad loaded the Kombi with the precision of a game of Jenga. Nothing was coming out of that boot until we reached the other end. It was wedged in tight.

We'd leave in the early hours of the morning. 'Time to wake up,' Mum whispered to each of us individually so she wouldn't wake Dad. And the eight of us got ready with heavy eyes in near silence. It was 3 am. We planned to 'get on the road,' as Dad would say, by 3:30. If we left by then, we could miss the traffic and the heat of the day and reach Aunty I's place (her name was Iris but everyone called her Aunty I) by about lunchtime. It was slightly thrilling to get up at that time of the day when the world was still and the air chilled your skin. We were excited about going away and at the same time fighting the lack of sleep. The last thing to do was wake Dad. Mum made sure he got as much rest as he could before the long journey.

North Haven was our heaven. Sand, sea, shells. The smell of salt water and eucalyptus. Christmas bells and flannel flowers. Dolphins playing through the waves. It was a holiday for us, but I know it was hard work for Mum. She still had to wash the clothes, but this time with a tiny twin tub washer instead of our usual 9kg top-loader, and she had to cook and clean for Aunty I as well as all of us kids. And there was no clothes dryer. Aunty I was hard work as she got older: she was Mum's mother's sister. She had always lived alone and was ten years older than we knew, we didn't discover that until after she died! Mum was so careful not to offend her, leaving the house cleaner than when we arrived. Aunty I was staunchly independent, I think that must run along the female line in our family!

Karuah was our halfway point. It was where we stopped for breakfast and a 'pitstop.' There was a picnic bench right on the river where we sat. Mum got out the green Tupperware container, filled with chicken sandwiches, some with butter, some without, some with mayonnaise, some without, some with iceberg lettuce, some with carrot, some with a combination of the above. Mum just knew the right amount of what we wanted. Dad stretched his legs and the 'little ones' ran around getting their giggles out. If there was a caravan alongside our spot at the river, Dad had a chat while Mum repacked the Tupperware container. Dad became really social and chatty when he was on holidays, like he did again when he retired.

Then the kids.

Dad was always last to get in, so he could maximise his leg-stretching time. They were such a team, my Mum and Dad. I always hoped I'd be part of a team like that one.

These holidays were such an adventure. And these places were such a long way away. The F1 started at Hornsby. When we were children, there was a toll collection point at Hornsby, not like the automated ones of today. Drivers had to stop and actually hand money to a person in a booth in the middle of the road. A real person. A human! With real money! Or if you had the exact amount, you could throw it into a bucket. Either way, you had to stop your vehicle. And whichever way it went, when we got all the way to Hornsby, we knew our holiday had begun. Hornsby was a long way away.

Hornsby was a world away. And Prof Herkes wanted to send me there.

Not for a holiday, but because my body didn't work. It was a crushing punishment.

In a ward like 7F, the population on any given day was usually older. Old. During my stay, I was the youngest lodger by half and then some, judging by the voice, the neck and the bare bottom. And being a neurology ward, we didn't all have the same ability to communicate, to move, to control our thoughts, our bladders, or our bodies. We were a motley crew, and at any time the nurses, doctors and therapists never knew what mixture they were going to be gifted with. They were always busy. I was glad I could ask for what I needed and didn't have to drool like Mr Helmet, with goop sliding down my front, or wander like Mr 90, flapping in the breeze. Or scream into the wind with no one answering, like poor old Mrs Next to Me. Or even worse, the ones I didn't notice. Who's to say the busy nurses had time to notice those who had no voice? Even with a voice, I didn't feel noticed. I sat in urine and filth.

Mum and Dad were with me one morning. It was the morning Prof Herkes told me I was leaving.

'It's a boy!' So many faces popped around the corner into my room announcing the news.

'Did you hear?'

'They had a prince!'

'Finally the baby's born!'

'Have you heard?'

'About 2:30. But they told the Queen first.'

'What do you think they'll call him?'

That became the next obsession for the world's media, the morning talk shows, and the man in the Union Jack suit on the side of the road outside the hospital. Knowing that I was being banished to Hornsby, I didn't care as much as I had before.

'I don't know. I just don't want it to be Alexander.' I wanted my Alex to be Alexander and I should've fought harder. I did make the case: 'He can choose to use either Alex or

Alexander. It gives him a choice.' I thought Alexander sounded distinguished. I should've spoken out louder.

Alex once said to me after he started school, 'I want to be Alexander.' He didn't know about my thoughts, I've never told him. He knew that we chose Alex because it was a strong name.

'You can be whoever you like,' I said.

Maybe it's because I was given a choice. You see, my first name is Mary, my middle name is Anne. I was named for Mum's and Dad's love of Mary Our Lady and her mother, Anne. My parents were people of great faith. Until I was born, they hadn't decided whether I would be Mary Anne or Anne Marie. They knew they would use the two names, without a hyphen, so that way I could decide as I got older whether I wanted to be known by one name or two. But I have always been Mary Anne. When I started high school, a couple of teachers began calling me Mary, but I corrected them. Although I was very shy, I always corrected my name. One of the boys I went to primary school with said to me one day, 'Why do they keep calling you Mary? You're Mary Anne.' He was right. I am Mary Anne.

Mum and Dad knew I was being moved that day and they wanted to see me before I went on my way. Mum packed the few things I owned in that room: a phone charger, a phone, the handbag I still had from the first day I arrived in the ambulance, a hairbrush and a headband. I wore my blue fleece jacket, my rings and my watch. I had nothing else. My clothes and shoes had been sent home. There was no point keeping them there, I couldn't walk in the shoes, I couldn't bend down to put them on. The clothes would have been filthy by now. So all I wore was the tie-back gown and a nappy.

'We don't call them nappies,' a nurse told me one day.

'Well what exactly are they?' I asked.

'We call them pads.'

They were nappies. Pull-ups. The same as the ones my babies wore to bed. I was wearing nappies. And it didn't really matter if I wore them or not. They still leaked through. I still sat in filth. The nappy kept some in, and the rest leaked out. I did have a colostomy bag at one stage. I think that was worse, where I had a clear plastic bag full of yellow wee dangling off the side of my bed for all the world to see. It was all awful.

Mum was horrified when she saw me pushing the button and no one came. Her face tried so hard not to show that she wanted to cry. She didn't cry, not in front of me, and neither did Dad. When the nurse finally came, Mum said, 'She's been pressing the button for ages. She's wet.' It was awful to hear Mum say that. More layers of dignity stripped away. I wanted to be strong for them, like I wanted to be strong for my children.

'Right. I hear we're off to Mt Wilga.' The patient transfer driver was upbeat. 'Sorry we're so late.' It was now the afternoon. We were going to catch the afternoon peak traffic.

'Name?'

'Date of Birth?'

'Do you know what day it is?'

'Who's the Prime Minister?'

What a ridiculous question. In Australia in 2013, the Prime Minister's job was a revolving door, we went through so many of them. Nobody could keep track of who the Prime Minister was.

He was pushing one of those narrow ambulance trolleys.

'O.K. We need to drop someone else off on the way. The traffic is pretty busy. You'll be there in about an hour.' My mood didn't match his. 'Up you get.'

This was the point at which Mum's usual calmness changed. She was seething. Her pale Irish skin turned through a few shades of purple, and it was all she could do not to jump across the room and attack that man.

'SHE CAN'T GET UP THERE! SHE CAN'T EVEN WALK! DIDN'T THEY TELL YOU! SHE CAN'T MOVE HER LEGS! YOU HAVE TO HELP HER!'

Thank goodness Mum was there. What a voice! Where had that been hiding all my life?

The Breakout

'We'll go back to Alex and Adelaide.' Mum and Dad were leaving.

'Tell them I love them,' I said through hidden tears. I waved like the Queen heading off to her waiting chariot.

'We will.'

We had time for the very briefest of hugs, and I was whisked away. Not really whisked, wheeled away. It was the fastest my nappy-wearing body had travelled in what felt like a lifetime. I was breaking out of there, but not going home. I was strapped on tight and my bag was shoved against my dead feet. It was a black leather backpack. Very practical. I was very practical.

Adelaide was a very early walker. She started walking long before she turned one. Alex was an early talker. He started talking a long time before he was one. They were a great team, if they needed something, Alex would tell Adelaide and she would go and get it. Until she decided she didn't like being told, and he decided he didn't like things being done for him. Then Alex started to walk, and Adelaide started to talk! So we had two early walkers and two early talkers.

I got the black leather backpack so both hands were free when we were out. They didn't like to stay in the pram from a very young age. As I said, I was very practical. My babies wore a lot of Bonds suits. They wore them everywhere, morning, noon and night. Comfortable, practical and easy to move in. It must have been a sight: two little babies, the same age, toddling around in their Bonds suits (different ones, they were always in different Bonds suits; they are different people), with their tiny little shoes on, arms stretched up forever holding my hands. Walking like professionals. The black leather backpack was a must. No fancy handbags would work in this situation. I had to be practical.

Today, the black backpack was as lifeless as my legs, as flaccid as my feet. It was ridiculous, squeezed against me. Why did I need it or its contents? My purse? I wasn't in need of money or cards. My car keys? I wasn't driving. My house keys? I wasn't going home. That bag was a stowaway on my journey to where I didn't want to go.

Dad stood at the door and Mum held her checked daddy hanky at her mouth. She waved it every now and again. They looked small as I coasted down the hall of 7F for the last time. There was nothing they could do.

I had a travel buddy that day in the Patient Transfer Vehicle. He was sitting on a seat, whereas I was strapped to the trolley. Ironically, he lived in Lane Cove.

'We'll just drop Charlie off first and then we'll head to Mt Wilga. It'll take about an hour. Traffic's pretty bad.'

I don't know if the old man's name was Charlie, but any time Mum got annoyed with a driver on the road, she would call them Charlie, like it was the worst word she could think of: 'What is this Charlie doing?' 'Come on, Charlie!' She didn't use it often, so when 'Charlie' came out, we knew she wasn't happy. And on this occasion, I was not happy.

This 'Charlie' was going home. I wanted to be going home. This 'Charlie' was walking. I wanted to be walking. As it turned out, this 'Charlie' was only just walking. He must have been almost a hundred. And the poor old fellow got out at a block of units where he lived all by himself. That gave me an excuse to cry. He got out of the Patient Transfer with the help of the paramedic, still wearing his hospital gown with his nappy underneath, and he walked to the apartment building, hunched over. They took him inside and then he was on his own. I imagined he was a Frequent Flyer. I decided I probably should change his name after that. He didn't deserve to be a 'Charlie.'

Like all the lovely, caring nurses, the fellow who sat in the back of the Patient Transfer vehicle with me tried to be upbeat and happy. So I pretended I was the same. But inside I screamed, 'Get me out of here! I need to go home!' We were so close to home. But even if we did go home, it would have been of no use: there were 26 steps from the road down to the house and another 26 from the house down to the laundry and the backyard. In my state, I might as well have been put in front of a brick wall and left there. I was annoyed again, 'Charlie' had a better chance of getting into my house than I did.

We drove along the Pacific Highway. They were right, the traffic was a bit of a nightmare. Because we were late, people were starting to head home from work. It was lucky it was July and school holidays; otherwise there would have been school zones everywhere. One minute it was a 60 zone, then 40. There was a bottleneck as people headed home away from the city, so we were only going 20. It was a really busy afternoon. Lying down and watching the traffic flash past made me feel sick in the pit of my stomach. My head felt like it was whizzing, there was that roller coaster again, and I hate roller coasters. Or maybe it was just not wanting to go.

The great big green road sign pointed right to Newcastle and the North Coast. That was the way we always followed to go to North Haven. That was the way I knew. But on this day, we followed the unknown sign straight ahead. It was the sign pointing to Hornsby. Other than a toll collection point, I was ignorant of what Hornsby was like. I didn't realise it was a busy metropolis with huge private schools and a massive shopping centre, with a car park entrance that looked like it was about to swallow us whole as we drove toward it.

We escaped the car park signs and continued on, past the doctors' practices, the ultrasound places, the many traffic lights, until we were spat out into suburbia. Normal houses. There was a driveway that just seemed to appear amongst the regular homes.

'Here we are. Mt Wilga. It's a great place. They'll look after you.'

And just like that, he was crawling to the back of the truck head first, opening the doors and blinding me with the sun that flooded in. I hadn't been outside for almost two weeks. It felt longer. My eyes weren't used to the burning of the outdoors. It made me sneeze. Twice. It was good to be out of the conditioned air of the hospital and breathing the real air of the outdoors. I could smell the eucalyptus trees, mixed with a little bit of car fumes from the car park. And even though I'd had a window with a view, my eyes were bursting with the 360-degree sights: trees to the sky, reflections coming off the cars, colours bright, people moving around. So many colours. So much movement.

The sounds were foreign too. The 'beeps' and 'drips' and constant calling out of Ward 7F were gone. Gone. Replaced with birds, chatter, laughter, cars starting, and a strange pop, pop, popping noise coming from the Rifle Range next to the car park.

My people trolley clunked out of the transfer truck and crunched onto the bitumen. I was pushed up the ramp, spun into the foyer of Mt Wilga Rehabilitation Hospital, and greeted by some lovely, welcoming ladies in very official navy and white uniforms. You never feel at your best or in your power when you're lying flat on your back, strapped to a trolley in a nappy you're not even sure is wet or dry. So I smiled politely and hoped they would hurry up and get me out of sight. I didn't like being the conspicuous one.

The transfer guys seemed to know people and said hello here and there as we wheeled along the wide corridors. If I had to say something good, it was that I could see outside. If I had to say something good. The windows were big and the place felt airy. The light didn't feel artificial. And it didn't feel like a place where people came to be sick. It felt more like a place where people came to get better.

My OT was lovely. Sharon. She was the one who met me in the room. She had a clipboard and a pencil and asked me lots of questions about why I was there, what I could do and feel, and how we were going to work together. I thought she said she was going to help me to 'get better', but looking back now, she wouldn't have said that. She would not have made that promise. I even thought she might have said 'try to get better', but I don't think she would have said that either, because to 'get better' would have implied there was something wrong with me the way I was. She was a professional. She would not have made that implication. If this was the best I had, she would have taught me to live with it. So I'm sure 'try to get better' are my words, and she probably said something more like, 'We're going to work together.'

Sharon listened to my story: 'It started with a heavy foot. I went to the hospital. They thought it was Guillain-Barré, but the neurologist worked out it was Transverse Myelitis.'

'You were seeing Geoffrey Herkes?'

'Yes.' By the way, she forgot to call him the Prof! 'Will he come here?'

'No. He's organised for you to see Grace Leong while you're here. She's wonderful. Then when you go home you can make an appointment to go back and see Geoff.'

Again, no Prof. She called him Geoff! 'Do you know how long I'll be here?'

'Well, that depends on how things go. Everybody is different. Anywhere from 12 weeks to 12 months.'

What? It was six weeks to six months before. My sentence had just doubled!

Mt Wilga

'One of us will be here for you to shower in the morning.'

'What do you mean?'

'One of the OT team will be here in the morning to shower you.'

'Can't I shower myself?'

'Not until we see how you go.'

Not again. I didn't really know how I was going to get to the shower on my own, but I didn't want someone watching me shower again.

I was given a brochure to peruse. It looked more like I was staying in a hotel than a hospital. There was a form to sign and a timetable of supports for the wall. There was a menu for the next day that looked like it came from a restaurant, interests, likes, dislikes, strengths, that sort of thing. Then I was questioned about the same old things: what was my name? When was my birthday? What was I doing there? What was the day of the week? Who was the Prime Minister?

When you've been in hospital for a long time and the days have been running into each other, answering a question like 'What is the day of the week?' becomes quite tricky, whether you have dementia or a brain injury or not. The days all become one. And as for 'Who is the Prime Minister?' At that time, Australia was in a situation where we had Kevin Rudd, then Julia Gillard, then Kevin Rudd again, and then Tony Abbott. In 2013, we had three Prime Ministers. It was like a revolving door. So to ask, 'Who is the Prime Minister?' became a bit of a running joke. It was hard to keep track.

My room looked nice enough. Beige. Beige floor. Beige walls. Beige doors. Beige curtains. Beige bed covering. Blah. There was no weekend painter walking the aisles of Bunnings here. Just beige. The huge hospital bed took up most of the space in the middle of the room. The message here was REST. Then the bedside table next to it, with a lockable top drawer. 'Make sure you lock up any valuables. Just in case. Here is the key.' Straight away I put my wallet in the top drawer and locked it. Just in case. My car key went in there. Just in case. And when I slept, I put my rings in there. Just in case. During the days, I wore my engagement ring and my wedding ring, most days.

They brought my dinner that night, which had been ordered by someone else the day before. I wasn't there, so I didn't get to order. The person who did order was lucky and got to go home, so they didn't need it. I got theirs. I don't remember what it was, but I do remember I didn't want it. I didn't want anything. It went back to the kitchen with apologies for the wastage, and hopefully no offence.

I got to order breakfast the next day and went with my usual: porridge, honey, and fruit. Best to stick with what you know. Shower time was awful. Sharon came back, her cheery self, armed with her clipboard, ready to take notes on what I could and couldn't do. 'Can't I just have a shower by myself?'

'Not until I see what you can do.'

So that was what I had to do, show them what I could do. That made me absolutely determined to prove that I could manage on my own, so I wouldn't have people watching me all the time. First, I had to get through this. Sitting on the shower chair, showing that I could wash myself, dry myself.

The hard part was getting dressed because I was stuck. I had no way of getting from the bathroom to the bedroom without help. I couldn't even lift my legs to get my knickers on. Sharon watched. It was obvious I couldn't do it.

'Do the bad leg first,' she said.

So I put the hole for the left leg on the ground, used my arms to yank my left leg into the air, and put it down into the top of the knicker hole. Then I did the same with the other side, manoeuvre the right hole to an easy position near my body, use my arms to lift my right leg, and drop it into the hole. Once both feet were sitting over the top of the correct holes, I could wriggle the knickers up my calves, over my knees, along my quads, under my bottom, and up towards my back.

What an effort.

And then there was the whole trying to put on a bra with only one good arm. The best thing to do was to do the clasps up at the front and spin it around to the back. I had to be careful how I did it because if I spun it too fast or too hard, the skin on my body would rip off with the bra.

That was an effort too.

It was great advice to always start with the worse side. If I started with the better side, there'd be no energy left to do the other side. I still start with the worse side.

To shower and dress in front of someone else was awful. I've never had great confidence in my body, gosh, I've never had any kind of positive confidence in my body. As a little girl at primary school, I was really quite oblivious to all things like that. I went along and was friends with everyone in my class, in my school.

The principal of my school wrote in my autograph book at the end of Year Six, 'You are always smiling. Keep smiling.' He was right, I was always smiling. I was a happy kid. There was no reason not to be happy. Mum and Dad gave us a wonderful childhood.

I was happy at high school. I loved the learning. I loved my friends. I loved the independence of having my own school, because there was no local Catholic high school when it was time for me to go. As a result, I went to a different school to my five sisters and two brothers. It gave me my own space. I loved it.

I caught the train to school. The train station at Windsor opened in 1864, but in the days I was at high school, things hadn't really changed much. The building was still the old convict bricks, the bullnose roof, and smokers on the platform. Most importantly, there were no electric trains to Windsor, we had to change trains in the middle of the journey. It was a diesel rail motor train from Windsor, then change at Riverstone, four stations later, for an electric train. I loved the trust Mum and Dad had in me, being allowed to catch the train.

But high school was also when I became more self-conscious, more body-conscious. Maybe we all did. That was the 1980s. I decided that I liked Jimbo (name changed for fear of his mortification) more than the other boys. We were in the same Year Six class, gosh, we'd been in most of the same classes since Year One. All of a sudden, I wanted to be one of his friends. I wanted to be his 'special friend.' I decided I liked him more than the other boys.

But guess what? Jimbo didn't like me more than the other girls. Jimbo didn't want to be one of my friends, and he definitely did not want to be my 'special friend.' Jimbo's friends thought it was hilarious. They were 12-year-old boys, of course they would. Jimbo's family thought it was hilarious too. His way of protecting himself was by making fun of me. He was awful, saying, 'She's fat. She's ugly. She's lard. I hate her.'

Every morning, I would be on the train when his friend Deano Bonnello (name is changed to protect the wicked here too), surrounded by his posse of other pimply 12-year-old boys, would greet me with, 'Hey Fat Mary Allen. What's happening, Fat Mary Allen?' (He didn't even get my name right.) Let me just say, Deano Bonnello wasn't much chop himself, but as a 13-year-old girl hearing those words through all those high school years, especially in front of Jimbo, that didn't matter. Those words stuck. They struck. Hard. And they still stick, all these years later.

The 53-year-old woman still looks in the mirror and sees 'Fat Mary Allen' on bad days. No matter how hard I try.

In the shower at Mt Wilga, I was Fat Mary Allen with someone watching me, and in my ears were Jimbo and Deano Bonnello and their band of pimply boys yelling, 'Hey Fat Mary Allen.' 'What's happening, Fat Mary Allen?' 'You're lard.' 'You're fat and ugly.' 'We hate you.'

That's pretty much how I felt about myself in that shower with eyes on me.

'Don't worry. We do this all the time.' Sharon tried to be comforting. Her words were the same as the nurse's at the hospital.

So was my reply: 'But I don't.'

After the rigmarole of the shower and getting dressed, the timetable for the day began. I was down for Occupational Therapy, Physiotherapy and Exercise Physiology.

'Would you like to speak to a psychologist?'

'No thanks.'

The first day at Mt Wilga started early, about 8:00. Mike brought me some real clothes. My own clothes from home. A nurse transferred me to a wheelchair. I didn't know where I was going, but I knew the timetable said 'Physiotherapy' and I knew there was a huge folder pushed down the back of the chair. The folder couldn't have much in it because I was new to this place. Surely the size of the folder wasn't an indication of how long I was going to have to be there.

I was parked with some other people in wheelchairs just inside the door of the gym. Not a gym with weights, gaudy-lit mirrors and people with perfect bodies and skimpy outfits. This one had polished boards on the floor, with coloured tapes marking different distances. There were bars down the length of the room that looked a bit like ballet barres, but this didn't look like a ballet studio. There were gigantic chairs that tilted backwards and poles that swung parallel to the ground. There was a hoist to lift someone out of a wheelchair and into another chair. It was mind-boggling to see. This was my world.

There were mirrors, but there weren't too many midriffs and muscle-bods looking back. Those mirrors told very different stories. There were boxes made of timber and foam, and there were plastic cups and coloured balls of all sizes, from golf balls to giant yoga balls. I was terrified to think what would be going on in there.

'I'm Ian. I'm your physio,' said a very tall, thin man with a strong Scottish accent. 'And I don't do tears.' He said it with a laugh. I tried to laugh back, but I'm quite sure some rogue tears escaped and trickled down my face. It wasn't because Ian scared me, it was because he was standing there on two legs that worked, and I was sitting there in a wheelchair with two that didn't, wanting to be at home with my children.

Mike was there to meet Ian. He was on his way to work. He said hello, dropped off a couple of clothes, and left.

'Okay. We're going to put this belt on you. We'll try the yellow one.' It was a thick white belt made of sturdy fabric, the height of my torso. It went all the way around my middle and velcroed together really tightly. There were yellow vertical handles on it. I learnt later that there were belts with red and green handles too. The colours indicated the sizes of the belts. Ian strapped the belt around me. 'Nice and tight.' He was on one side of me and someone else was on the other.

'Ready?' They checked the brakes on the wheelchair and pulled me up into the air, right up on my wobbly legs. They were ready to collapse underneath me.

'Right then, we're going to go for a little walk.'

'But I can't feel my legs.' My head spun. I was floating.

'That's okay. Let's go.' I had to remind myself that Ian didn't do tears.

And off we went.

The physiotherapists at Royal North Shore had visited a few times and introduced me to a thing called the Forearm Support Frame. It was a gargantuan thing with spidery legs.

It had moulded pads on the top where you lean your forearms, hence the name. It stood about three-quarters of my body height. I had to stand inside it and lean on the pads. Then I basically pushed it with the top of my body and my lower half trailed behind. It had these little things on the bottom at the front that looked like snow skis, so it sort of glided along the floor. It was just as well it didn't have wheels, because I would've shot along like a bullet!

No one had expected me to actually walk with one foot in front of the other since Craig told me to get into the ambulance on the 15th of July. That felt like a lifetime ago.

Until Ian. Ian just expected me to walk. The majority of my body had no feeling, it was just numb. I was sort of like a floating head with a right arm waving in the breeze. I didn't feel light; I felt like a head attached to a dead weight in the wind. My left thumb and pointer finger worked, but that was it. So when Ian said, 'Walk,' it felt a bit like Jesus telling Lazarus to 'Rise!' And had I walked, it would've been just as much of a miracle!

But the human body and the human brain are amazing. Someone explained to me that Transverse Myelitis is like a car crash in your spinal cord. When there's a car accident, the traffic needs to find new ways around the scene of the accident to get to and from its destination. Transverse Myelitis leaves lesions or blockages on your spinal cord, in my case, from T8 to C4, which means the messages can't get from your brain to your lower body or from your lower body to your brain. My brain might tell my body that I want to walk, but because of the blockage on my spinal cord, the legs wouldn't obey. Or I might put my left hand in hot steam without looking, and the message wouldn't get sent to my brain.

In years gone by, the medical field believed that if there was damage to the spine or brain, it was permanent. In other words, if you had a stroke, a head injury, or something like Transverse Myelitis, that was how you'd stay for the rest of your life. Thankfully, that thinking has changed. Brian, the Social Worker at Mt Wilga, suggested that I read Norman Doidge's book The Brain That Changes Itself. Not exactly light reading, but very interesting. I read it while I was in rehab. Some of the experiments that were done on animals, even on humans, in the early days of brain research would definitely not be allowed today. But today's findings stand on the shoulders of that research.

Ian threw down the Lazarus challenge: 'Walk!' So I was going to. Call me stubborn, or determined, or pig-headed, whatever it was, it's what got me going.

'Show me how.' And Ian would lift his leg. 'Show me again.' And he would lift his leg again.

'Show me a step.' Ian took one step. Slow motion.

'Show me your hip.' I watched his hip. Slow motion.

'Show me your knee.' I watched his knee. Slow motion.

'Show me your ankle.' I watched his ankle. Slow motion.

'How do your toes move?' He showed me his toes. Back and forth.

Over and over and over. Day after day after day. Morning, noon, Monday to Friday.

I heard Mum's voice, 'Just do it. Even if you can't feel it. Imagine it in your head.'

Over and over. I practised in the gym with my yellow handle around my waist. Ian on one side, someone else on the other. And I practised lying on my bed, sitting in my chair.

Then in the gym wearing my belt, just with Ian.

I practised pacing my bedroom, not allowed to leave until I was given the all clear. I walked laps around that bed, picturing my toes, ankles, knees, thighs, hips in my mind. I was a head moving around. I was a head to be reckoned with!

I was moving!

My body, never very good at sport, was moving! Was conquering the most important sport of all! Surviving. Learning how to walk … for the second time in my life.

By now I was allowed to shower on my own. I was finally gaining some independence, some dignity back. I was starting to feel more like myself. Although I was still locked away in a place where everything was done for me, and most of my neighbours were over seventy and happy to sit in a chair in the corner of their room buying vowels on *Wheel of*

Fortune, or catching up with friends on *The Young and the Restless*, or just sleeping through all the daytime hours. I felt like a caged lion. I wanted to pace, except I wasn't allowed out of my room, and I wasn't really pacing, I was more wobbling. Anyway, I wasn't allowed to pace!

It was exhausting. Every day I was wheeled to the gym. Every day I stood, sat, stood, sat. Over and over. So much repetition. Every day I did steps holding that ballet barre, looking nowhere near as elegant, but every single step, every little movement was so much more important than any leap in the air. Every step was getting me closer to home. They say if you want to become an expert at something, you need to do at least 10,000 hours of practice. I was well on my way.

The time came to take the belt off. The security blanket was going. The belt had been there to catch me if I fell. It wasn't going to be there any more. Ian still stood next to me, but it meant I didn't have handles any more. He trusted me enough to let go. At first, I didn't trust myself as much as he did. Like all the other days, Ian took one step. I took a step. A tentative step.

I watched his hip. I moved my hip. A tentative move.

I watched his knee. I bent my knee. A tentative bend.

I watched his ankle. I creaked my ankle. A terrified creak.

He showed me his toes. My toes didn't really move. But I pictured them in my mind.

I plonked along with heavy, flat feet. I was moving. My version of walking. Day after day I was getting faster, stronger, more confident.

It started to feel like I was wearing socks. Not just any socks, concrete socks. Knee-high concrete socks that squeezed my calf muscles and tightened as I moved. These concrete socks were lined with barbed wire, all the way down the inside. Can you imagine how comfortable that was? There was nothing underneath the feet, but all the way from the back of the knee to the ankle were these new sensations.

We started on a new medication protocol. I was taking Lyrica. It took the edge off, but it made me so tired. I wondered if these sensations meant the messages were getting through the damaged spinal cord. I hoped that was what it meant. I hoped the car crash had been cleared and traffic could pass as easily and freely as it had for the past forty-two years.

But that was not the case. The messages had found a new way to get around, and the new passages to and from the brain were going to be more rocky, painful, full of cramps. I was Ben Grimm turning into The Thing from *The Fantastic Four*. Except Thing had superhuman strength. 'Spastic limbs are weak limbs,' said Dr Leong when we looked at how stiff my legs were. The new tightness under the knees was getting worse with each day. Even though the traffic could pass through the site of the crash in my spine, it didn't get through easily.

Thing didn't have weak limbs. But my body felt like it had turned to stone. Even though feeling was coming back, it wasn't the right feeling. It was tight and sharp and heavy. My body was made of concrete and stone. And barbed wire. And any time something touched me, it was like glass slicing through the skin.

How was it that I couldn't feel things, but I could feel that?

Daily visits to the Occupational Therapist included things like using my right hand to pick up one clothes peg from an ice-cream container. I lifted the peg, opened it and pegged it onto a small string resembling a dollies' clothesline, all while sitting in my wheelchair. When I was successful, I could celebrate by picking up another peg from the ice-cream container, lift that peg and peg it onto the string. When I'd pegged six pegs onto the string, I could use my right arm to take each peg off the string and put them back into the container.

Next it was time to repeat the task with my left arm. How hard could it be? I had two-year-old twins and a husband at home. I washed clothes and hung them on the line all the time. I did basket loads every day. I carted those baskets up and down steps at home to get from the house down to the laundry underneath, and then to the backyard. Seven days a week. I was an Olympian clothes washer! This was six little coloured pegs in an ice-cream container on a table. And I could do it while sitting down.

But this was my new left arm. This was my brain sending messages around a car wreck. The left hand went into the ice-cream container. Check.

The fingers picked up the peg. Check.

Now to squeeze the peg open. That was a slightly different story. The fingers didn't get the message to do that job. They were a bit confused. The thumb and pointer knew what to do, but they were weak and needed the help of the other fingers.

It was hard to get those six little clothes pegs onto that line with my left hand. And exhausting. That had implications for other things: what about typing? My career depended on writing. I had always been a teacher. That was all I ever wanted to be. Ever since I was very little, I knew I was going to be a teacher.

When I was in kindergarten, my uncle said, 'Well, Professor, what are you going to be when you grow up?' He was trying to be funny because I had brought home a page of writing that surprised them all.

'I'm going to be a ballerina.' I was adamant. I had never tried ballet, nor did I know anyone who had ever tried ballet, but what else would a five-year-old say? Look at those outfits and just watch those lifts. Wouldn't any little five-year-old girl want to do that? That was my answer. 'I'm going to be a ballerina.'

But from about the age of six, I knew I was going to be a teacher, and as I grew older and could sort out my thinking realistically, I knew I was going to be a primary teacher and study at the Castle Hill Teachers College, which changed to the Australian Catholic University while I was there. I came from a long line of teachers. I don't know if that had an impact on me. Mum was a teacher, as was her sister, their mum and even her mother's aunties and uncle . I'm not sure about generations before that, but it wouldn't surprise me. No one was going to change my mind.

But someone did change my mind. 'Aim higher. You've got the marks. Don't waste them.' The careers adviser in Years 11 and 12 convinced me that I should strive higher. I started at Macquarie University in an Arts/History degree.

I hated it. I hated the travel, I hated the grey buildings, I hated that I was doing the wrong course. I should have been doing Primary Teaching like I'd always wanted. I felt out of place. I called ACU a few weeks after starting there.

'You'll need to come in for an interview.'

'That's OK.'

'What was your HSC score?' I told them.

'No, not the raw score, the scaled score.'

'That was my scaled score.'

'Can you come for an interview tomorrow?'

I started the next Monday, halfway through Semester 1. I never looked back. I loved everything about university. I loved teaching.

But I needed my fingers to be able to type.

What about playing the piano?

I started playing the piano when I was in Year 3. Mum found a lady in the local Gazette named Miss Valentini who lived around the corner from our primary school. She lived in the most beautiful, otherworldly Victorian cottage with a heritage order on it, set amongst other lovely little cottages. This section of George Street was built around 1794 by the well-to-do of the Windsor colonial set. Miss Valentini's house was surrounded by a low brick fence with a wrought iron gate that matched the ironwork on her front verandah. The verandahs were perfect places to watch the world pass by, and you didn't really realise how perfect until you stood there and actually watched. The house was a pretty, incredibly pale pink stucco over convict bricks.

Miss Valentini's music room was so quiet, there was no sound from outside until a bus stopped at the kerbside bus stop. Her walls were white with tiny musk-coloured roses printed on woodblock wallpaper. The focus was the fireplace with its glazed black and blue tiles. The floor shone like a mirror and, in pride of place, stood the piano. Positioned to the side of the double windows for maximum light was the polished oak Steinway, glowing, wearing the light from the street.

Learning to play those keys opened the world to another language. It meant concentrating on nothing but the notes and the counting and the feel of the ivory under my fingertips, the smoothness as my fingers danced across the keys. Maybe that was my chance to be a ballerina?

When I was ten, I entered the Hawkesbury Eisteddfod. The Doll's Lullaby was a pretty little piece by an 18th-century composer named Cornelius Gurlitt. I practised and practised, and as the day drew closer, of course, I practised harder, more like I should have. Miss Valentini was very good at breaking our pieces up into sections and showing us how to work on small sections until they flowed. Maybe play one section really loud or another really slow or staccato, until there was better control of the basic piece. It must've driven my family crazy to hear me practise as that Eisteddfod day approached!

Dad was at work and Mum was taking someone to the dentist, so it was just my sister and me that day. I played my little fingers loudly and quietly, fast and slow, however Mr Gurlitt instructed from the 1700s, in my brand-new pink Eisteddfod dress with the bow at the back. It was a relief to be finished and to sit in the audience to clap for the winners.

'It was very close between first and second place. Only one and a half points. Second place, with a score of eighty-six and a half, is The Doll's Lullaby.'

I continued to clap.

'That's you!' I was elbowed in the arm. 'That's you!'

I didn't really know what to do. It was the first time I had ever won anything, and what a thing to win! The pink bow at the back of what now became known as my 'Eisteddfod dress' trailed behind me on the way to that stage. I proudly accepted the little gold medal, bearing the symbols of the Hawkesbury, attached to the red ribbon. It sat on a certificate and a report. My head was in a bit of a daze. I didn't realise it was me until I was elbowed in the arm. 'That's you!' I'll never forget it.

I needed my fingers to be able to play. All of them.

If squeezing those clothes pegs was such a challenge, how would the task of using individual fingers, like typing letters on a keyboard, or making music on a piano work? What would be the challenge there?

I started to think about the Norman Doidge book. If the brain could change itself, how could I strengthen it to make sure I could type? How could I clear the car wreck?

I decided I would knit. I had some knitting needles and wool at home—nothing exciting. I was teaching Adelaide and Alex how to do Knitting Nancies. I used to be able to knit when I was young. I could crochet squares too, but I'd forgotten how to do that. My friend Sandra is great at crocheting. Every time there's a baby in her family, she makes amazing creations, clothes, booties, even a blanket in the shape of a cow to rest over the new baby's cot. She's very clever.

I asked to have my knitting needles and wool with me. And I knitted. It was very slow and loopy and loose at first, but it strengthened my fingers. And it was relaxing. Aunty I (Iris from North Haven) had beautiful embroidery skills. She used to stitch onto handkerchiefs and doilies, even tablecloths. She tried to show me some of the stitches once: daisy stitch, chain stitch, blanket stitch, long stitch. But at the time I was too young and wasn't really interested. I loved cross-stitch and still do, but it would be nice if I could ask Aunty I to teach me those beautiful embroidery skills now.

Death is so final. Once someone has gone from our family, all the wisdom from that person is gone forever. Not just the embroidery stitches, but the important life lessons. And you can guarantee that when someone is gone, we'll always think of something we want to know. It's too late when they're gone.

It was a good thing my right hand was always the dominant one.

Down the Aisle

Being without my babies was like being without my limbs. Part of me was missing. The world was not right, they were not with me, and I was not with them. We were the Three Musketeers. We had never been apart.

I could not visit them, and they could not even visit me.

'Tell them I love them,' I said to Mike one night on the phone.

'No,' he said with finality.

'What?' I was horrified.

It hit me like a brick to the stomach. I thought he would have been telling them I loved them every night, something like, 'Mummy loves you.' But no. I was simply a void.

'Why not?'

'It's too hard.'

Too hard? Too hard for who? Too hard in what way? I couldn't believe it, and I couldn't let it go.

'What do you mean?'

'They get too upset and they want you.'

Well, tell them where I am. Tell them I'm OK and tell them I'll be coming home. And bring them to see me!

Imagine what it must have been like for them. They went to sleep one afternoon like every other day, which they never liked, and they woke up, and for the first time in over two years, I wasn't there. I was gone. Just gone. And not only was I not there, I didn't come back. For ages. Sure, they saw me at Royal North Shore for a quick visit, sitting in a chair surrounded by cords and dripping sounds in the dark, but then nothing.

Until Mike finally decided he would bring them to see me. It was nearing the end of my time at Mt Wilga, I know because Barbara, Mike's mum, was with him.

'Merry Christmas,' she wrote in her Christmas letter to friends and family that year. *'Mary Anne's been in hospital, it's been nice because I've been able to spend time with the twins.'*

I found the letter on her computer that Mike got after she died.

It was another punch to the face.

Mary Anne's been in hospital, it's been nice.

I had to read it again. Nothing about it was nice.

Remember at the start, I wasn't going to go home, they were going to *make me comfortable*. Then after that, after I survived, I was expected to go home in a power chair to a home with fifty-two steps. However was that going to be 'nice'?

A real punch to the face. That, and her telling my mum that my children would be better off moving up to Yamba with her.

Another sock to the face.

One to the left. One to the right.

Smack. Smack.

Everyone at Mt Wilga knew they were coming to visit. Everyone at Mt Wilga knew all about them. Of all my achievements, my studies, my career attainments, my travels, of all the things I have ever done, my babies were and are my greatest source of pride. They are not perfect. None of us is perfect. But I love them for how they are and who they are.

Because I hadn't had visitors from home, I hardly had any clothes. It also meant I didn't have a regular washing service. There was a laundry down the hallway from my room, so I saved up my clothes until I had a bundle that needed washing and put them on my wheelie walker, trundling down the corridor. I washed the clothes, then went back to put them in the dryer, then back again to get them out.

It didn't take long before I got sick of wearing the same two outfits. So I got onto the World Wide Web. I was very familiar with the sizes at Blue Illusion. I looked through their catalogue and ordered a blue dress, a red dress, a couple of tops to go underneath and two pairs of leggings. There was no point having them sent to our house, so I had them sent to Mt Wilga.

I didn't think anything of it, but apparently the staff thought it was pretty ingenious. They couldn't believe it!

'It looks like you've got a gift.'

'Oh no. I ordered some things.'

'You ordered some things?'

'Yes.'

'To come here?'

'Yes.'

'What did you order?'

'Clothes.'

They just couldn't seem to get their heads around the fact that someone would order something to arrive there. My little bundle of internet shopping became the talk of the town!

Adelaide and Alex were supposed to be arriving at 11:00, Saturday morning. I was ready and waiting. And when you're waiting, any minute past the time seems like forever. I made sure I was wearing one of my old faithfuls, not one of my new purchases. I wanted to look like I did when I was at home with them.

I remember exactly what I was wearing, black tights, a black skivvy, and a woollen dress with a multitude of flowers designed in blacks and greys, finished with sequins. It sparkled in the light, and the three of us used to play with the little beads when they caught the sun. It was one of those things, you had to be really careful not to pull the beads and sequins too hard or they'd come off, and eventually there'd just be the plain black and grey fabric left. After all, it was the sparkles that made it extra special.

Getting socks on was nearly impossible, still is, but I had black socks on and black flat Velcro shoes.

My room was right at the end of a very long corridor, so the aisle made a great runway. At first, there was a quiet stampede of four little feet. I poked my head around the corner, just outside the door. The two brightest little faces, in the most mismatched outfits you've ever seen, came tearing towards me at a pace never before witnessed within the walls of that establishment! They were lightning-bolt fast, with smiles from ear to ear and laughs that would melt the hardest hearts.

Heads popped out of doorways to see what was going on, and when they saw the two little bodies streak past, they knew exactly what it was, my visit from Adelaide and Alex.

I waited at my door with my arms stretched out.

I caught them in the biggest, softest, most wonderful hug.

We were together again.

Until I saw, over their little heads, that I was going to have to share them with Mike's mum. I was angry. From the top of my head to the bottom of my numb feet. I hadn't seen them for months, and I thought maybe I could just have them to myself.

So I took them for a walk. Just the three of us.

I was only allowed to walk at that stage with my trusty four-wheel walker. I didn't like it, but it was the rule. I hated that I was supposed to use those wheels for support. I hated that they thought I couldn't do it on my own. But it was the rule. And if it meant I could go, I would use it.

I was embarrassed that I had to use it. Alex and Adelaide spied it in my room. They weren't embarrassed. They were two and a half, and they were impressed! It was a new contraption like Mama's (that was their name for my mum), and it meant a new toy for them. They sat on the seat, facing me. I pushed, and off we went.

Down the aisle we trundled. Giggling, turning heads. I'm sure there were a few tears shed along the way.

The last time I walked an aisle with such absolute joy was our wedding day, the second of September 2006. I didn't really know if I would ever get married. I guess, compared to all my friends, I was an ancient bride. I had accepted the role of bridesmaid with pride, seven times! Seven times! What an honour. I didn't really think it would ever be my turn. But our day came.

I didn't find it stressful; there were people who knew what they were doing, so I asked them to help. Ann created magic with the flowers, Christine made our hair look gorgeous, Sonia did wonders with our make-up, Vera and the choir from school sounded heavenly, Leanne was the most elegant MC ever, and the cake makers had never made wedding cakes before, but we knew they could do it.

All I really had to do was look beautiful. And for the first time in my life, I knew I did. I wanted to look like Audrey Hepburn at the races in My Fair Lady, long sleeves, a high neck and a pure white, lacy, straight dress. I knew that was how I wanted to look.

I looked the exact opposite!

I walked that aisle at St Matthews in the biggest, most stunning dress (without lace), which was actually a skirt and top, with sparkles across the bodice. I walked that aisle with dreams of walking towards the man I was going to be with forever. Of living together 'in sickness and in health, till death do us part'. Of sitting on a verandah like Miss Valentini's as a wrinkly old couple, talking about our grandchildren and reflecting on our day.

Sometimes the courageous thing is recognising that the sickness and health part isn't working. But not when I was walking down that aisle. It was the same aisle my mum and dad had walked down for their wedding. I'm sure their marriage wasn't always perfect, but they were married for fifty years when Mum died. And they were together through everything.

When I walked that aisle on that most beautiful day, I dreamt that Mike and I would be like Mum and Dad. I hoped that we would be like Mum and Dad. That was a magical aisle to walk down.

The Mt Wilga aisle didn't have the beautiful stained glass windows, and I certainly wasn't wearing the stunning wedding gown, crystal tiara and trailing veil. Although I did have sparkles. And I had as much love as I did that day when I was bursting with joy as a bride, and the faces at the other end had as much love and hope as any bridegroom on his wedding day waiting to make the vow, 'I will be here in sickness and in health, till death we will part.' They were my little crutches.

When I got home from Mt Wilga, I told myself how clever I was that I could walk all by myself.

'No, I don't need a stick.

No, I don't need a crutch.

Or a walker.

Or a chair.'

And I was right. I didn't need any of those aids.

Until Alex and Adelaide started at pre-school.

You see, that's when I discovered the truth: they were my little crutches. The faces at the end of the aisle. They had been holding my hands, one on each side, keeping me steady. When I lost my little anchors, I lost my balance. I couldn't do it on my own. I had to accept that I needed help.

And admitting that took a lot of strength.

Just Popping In

'Are you sure you wouldn't like to speak with the psychologist?' I was asked so many times.

I was adamant. I did not want to speak to the psychologist. I had never in my life felt the need to speak with one. The only experience I'd had with psychologists was through referring families at school, and those family psychology appointments we'd had many years earlier. They were horrid sessions where it felt like every innocent someone was being blamed for something they had absolutely nothing to do with. Those sessions caused more pain and suffering than any good, by far.

There was absolutely no way in the world I wanted to speak with a psychologist and risk making an already horrible situation even worse.

'Hi. I'm Rob. I'm just walking past. Thought I'd pop in and say hello.'

I already knew the OT team. He wasn't one of them. I knew all of the physios, he wasn't from there either. I knew the cleaners and the dinner ladies (and they were all ladies), and the medication nurses. Rob wasn't any of those people. I had just met the social worker, a new face talking to me about going home, Brian, discussing services I might be able to access when I got there. He mentioned applying for the Total and Permanent Disability Insurance through my superannuation. I have to admit, it was something I had never heard of. It was one of those things in the parallel universe we were often oblivious to, because we didn't need to know about it.

'Oh, I don't need to worry about that, but thank you.' That didn't apply to me. That was for people with total and permanent disabilities. I was sure I was going to get better. In fact, I was convinced that each day I was going to wake up cured. Every day I didn't wake up 'fixed' was a surprise.

'I'm Rob. Just walking past. Thought I'd pop in and say hello. I'm one of the psychologists here at Wilga. Brian mentioned you to me.'

'Oh.'

He was a young fellow, very friendly, nothing like the scary family psychologist my family had met all those years ago in that dark office in Pennant Hills. That's not my story to tell, so I'll leave it at that. Rob was easy-going, and it really did feel like he just wanted to have a chat.

'How are you feeling?'

I always answered the same: 'I'm well, thanks.' Even when the pain was roaring and the skin was burning. I always said it with a smile. I'm sure that, to look at me, people wouldn't really have known that there was anything wrong. They would, however, have noticed the weight gain very quickly, because that miracle drug, Lyrica, was a double-edged sword, it held off a teensy bit of the agony but added to the girth.

'Welcome back, Fat Mary Allen,' I heard the whispers from my teenage years.

Rob popped his head around the corner once, and then he started popping around the corner regularly, 'just to say hello and see how things are going'. He had a way of starting up a conversation.

I always seemed to come back to the same thing: 'How am I going to help Mike cope with things the way they're going to be now? How will I help him cope with our new normal?' We never talked about how I was going to cope, I guess it was just assumed I would. The conversation was always, 'How will I help Mike?'

One of our 'just popping around the corner' conversations touched on whether I was angry about what had happened.

'No. Not angry. Just sad. Everything about it is sad. I have lost my body. I have lost so much time with my children. It's like they've been ripped away from me. I haven't been able to see them or talk to them or touch them or cuddle them. They're babies. They're part of me, and it feels like they're gone.'

'They're not really gone.'

'It feels like they're gone. I saw them once at Royal North Shore. I've seen them once here at Mt Wilga, and I had to share them with Mike's mum. Mike won't even tell them that I love them over the phone.'

'What do you mean?'

'When I say "tell them I love them," Mike says "no", and when I ask why not, he says because it's too hard. Too hard? Too hard is being torn away from your babies and not knowing when or if you're going to get back to them. Too hard is not knowing your own body. Too hard is losing your whole identity and having to find a whole new you. When you ask me if I'm angry, I can honestly say no, I'm not angry. I'm sad. Everything about this is sad.'

'I guess there are some things for which I am grateful. I'm grateful it didn't happen to Mike, because I know he would not have coped. I am so grateful it didn't happen to Alex or Adelaide, because it would be devastating to see this happen to my babies at the beginning of their lives, and it was a relief it wasn't Mum or Dad, because the toll it takes on a body is too much, and I just can't imagine what it would be like for someone their age. Regardless, it is sad.'

It was just so sad.

My chats with Rob, and my subsequent chats with Kim, my psychologist on the outside, have changed my attitude to psychologists. I think everyone should have access to a good, strong psychologist. I think it's important that we don't wait until we need to speak with someone; it's important to have a positive relationship with a psychologist, like we do with a GP. If we could take away the stigma around talking with a psychologist, maybe more people would access their services.

It's also important to know it's okay to find the right fit. That family psychologist we used to have to see was an awful situation for our family, but she was recommended. When I first spoke to someone after Rob, she was definitely not the right person: too young and giggly. I went to someone else. Kim. She challenges me and sometimes says things I might not like to hear, but our values align, and she feels like my own brain at its strongest and most confident.

Music

The gym was different to the rest of Mt Wilga. It was noisy. There was shouting, cheering, squeaky shoes and balls bouncing. There was always Ian's Scottish lilt. People were encouraged to move around. And the moving around looked different for each of us. For me, when I first got there, my 'moving around' was a friendly fellow pushing my very stiff, very unhappy body in a wheelchair, led by a face that tried to be strong while masking a sadness that could not be described.

And there was always music.

It was like there was Mt Wilga, and then there was the gym. It was its own little world. Like everywhere else at Mt Wilga, there were huge windows that let in the view and the light. It didn't feel like a hospital. It was bright. There was easy access to the outside, with a grassy hill where we could do desensitisation work. That was really hard, because every blade of grass felt like a shard of glass slicing into my flesh.

The first morning in the gym was silent, except for: 'I'm Ian, and I'll be your physio, and I don't do tears,' in that Scottish accent.

After that, there was always music. The music made it easier to move. It was funny because there were some songs that seemed to play every day, the ones that were popular in the second half of 2013.

There was the pulsing and pounding of Hey Brother by Avicii. Every day I heard it. Sometimes more than once a day, because I'd hear it when I was in the gym and then again when I was walking past. The speed of the music was fast, faster than a walking pace, probably more of a jogging speed, like 100-time on the metronome. It was bouncy. Every time I heard it, I wanted to jump, and I was not good at jumping! It was catchy because the words were slower, easy to understand. They juxtaposed with the beat. You could feel the musicians playing quavers, but the singer seemed to be singing minims. The pitch was low, sung by men, in the bass. Easy to sing along with. I always said I had a 'boy voice', because I could speak but not sing, even after doing singing lessons.

Mum and all of her family had such beautiful singing voices. Her father was born in Fiji, the son of a British tea company owner. 'They have music in their souls,' he used to say of the Fijians. 'Music in their souls.'

I used to sing to Adelaide and Alex, and we used to have great fun dancing, but I was never confident at either. When they were babies, although it was so special that they were twins, it was important for me to maintain their individual identities, even down to having their own bedtime song.

I used to sing Alex All My Loving every night. It used to give me goosebumps, and my eyes burned with tears every time I sang the line, 'Close your eyes and I'll kiss you, tomorrow I'll miss you.' I just couldn't help myself. Even thinking about it now, with my fourteen-year-old baby walking around with his big man voice and hairy legs, I want to cry. Just try thinking of someone you love at the end of the day: 'Close your eyes.' See them in their vulnerability: 'and I'll kiss you.' And imagine not seeing them the next day: 'tomorrow I'll miss you.'

Heartbreaking.

Adelaide's song was Somewhere Over the Rainbow from The Wizard of Oz, except I kept forgetting the order of the verses, so I'd just jumble them up and make my own version. It was always a lovely version, just not necessarily the same one. Adelaide liked it. Even now, she sometimes still wants me to sing it when she feels down. And why wouldn't you want to think about a world where bluebirds fly, where you can wish upon stars, and where all your troubles melt like lemon drops?

Adelaide has always loved drawing and painting and all things art and craft. And colour. I didn't know that when she was a tiny baby, but that song about a rainbow was a perfect fit.

In retrospect, both songs were. Of course they were both old songs. They both had so much passion without being overtly passionate. They each belonged to someone. I wonder if, somewhere hidden in their minds, there's a memory of those sounds.

Not just in my mind, but hidden in my whole body, is the sound of that song, Hey Brother, and the days I heard it at Mt Wilga. Any time those notes and words enter my ears, the beats move my body. I can't forget it. The first line of the song was one of those lines that really meant something. It certainly meant a lot to me in my situation at the time:

Hey brother, there's an endless road to rediscover.

There sure was an endless road to rediscover. I just did not want that road to involve a power chair!

In 2013, I was coming to the end of my maternity leave and family leave, and Mike was desperate for me to return to work. From Mt Wilga, I called Head Office to see if I could apply to do my Assistant Principal position part-time.

'It's never been done before. You'd be a trailblazer.'

I was too tired and in too much pain to blaze any trails.

'You can take unpaid sick leave.'

So I opted for that. I still believed I was going to get better. What was I thinking?

'Are you sure you wouldn't like to meet with the psychologist?'

Still no, thanks.

Surprisingly, the psychologist happened to come by my room, just coincidentally, of course.

'Just thought I'd pop in to say hello. How are things?'

We continued to chat.

And chat.

And chat a bit more.

And it was always about the same thing: "How will I help Mike cope with the changes?" You would think maybe it would have been about learning to cope with life without my career, or learning to live in a body that doesn't work sexually, or learning to be a mum to two very young children in a new body, or how I would return home after being in hospital for three months, or how to help my mum now that Dad had his bypass. But no. "How will I help Mike cope with a disabled wife?" I was as ignorant of my own needs as the unhelpful neighbour.

The other song that took the world by storm in 2013, played in the gym every day on high rotation, was Katy Perry's Roar!

I got the eye of the tiger, a fighter

Dancing through the fire

Cause I am a champion, and you're gonna hear me roar

Louder, louder than a lion

Cause I am a champion, and you're gonna hear me roar!

You held me down but I got up.

What a celebration song that was! When I got home from Mt Wilga, we made long, sparkling streamers out of crepe paper and glitter paper, and attached them to cardboard rolls (not toilet rolls, teachers know that would be unhygienic for craft purposes!).

The wonderful, colourful liquid rainbows were like peacock tails plucked from the sky. We shook them and danced with them, making up the most perfect routines that burst into the air when Katy Perry sang ROAR! Arms started down on the ground, with streamers hidden in still piles, until they magnificently erupted into the air with the energy of the tiger we were singing about. Adelaide and Alex jumped and ran around the house, and I clomped along as much as I could. We all ended up red-faced as beetroots, glowing like our streamers, ready to collapse at the end of the song, but all happy to go for another round.

These songs were perfect for the gym. Their speed, pitch and tone made the work easier, and their words pushed me on and on.

Later on, when I was working through the day program in 2015, the most powerful song yet played. It started as a very meek and mild, quiet song, one you could almost miss if you weren't paying attention:

Like a small boat on the ocean

Sending big waves into motion

Like how a single word

Can make a heart open

I might only have one match

But I can make an explosion

And just when you've been lulled into thinking this is a quiet, sleeping little tune, BANG! It hits you between the eyes with the full force of Muhammad Ali's boxing glove:

And all those things I didn't say

Were wrecking balls inside my brain

I will scream them loud tonight

Can you hear my voice tonight

So now you're thinking, okay, I had better listen to this person; they might have something to say. After all these years, I am finally speaking out about what happened to my body, mind and family, starting on that Absolutely Ordinary Day in July 2013. At first, I was a small boat on the ocean, but now, with gusto:

This is my fight song

Prove I'm alright song

My power's turned on

Starting right now I'll be strong

I'll play my fight song

And I don't really care if nobody else believes

Cause I've still got a lot of fight left in me

What an anthem! Rachel Platten's The Fight Song.

It has all been a fight. Every single day and night is a fight. Lying in bed is a fight, because I haven't been able to roll over since 14th July 2013, the day before transverse myelitis entered my body. Being awake is a fight to know what my body is doing, to make sure other people don't bump into me and knock me down. It is a fight to let people know I am trying my hardest.

Sometimes it is a fight against strangers, sometimes against people I know. Sometimes it has been a fight against people I love. Sometimes, it is a fight against myself and my own body.

But I am strong, stubborn, independent, and a person of faith. And my power's turned on!

Contact With The Outside

Hornsby felt like such a long way away. Although it wouldn't have mattered where I was. If I was locked in that hospital – or any hospital – and I was next door but not within reach of my children, it would've felt like a world away. I missed my babies as if limbs had been torn off me. Any time I spoke to Mike, of course, I asked him how they were and what they were doing.

He had so much help. Really, except for the night times, his life continued on as it always had. He worked during the week, went out on the weekends. Like I said, the neighbour told me, *'It was hard for Mike living with a disabled wife.'*

It was an embarrassment.

I was an embarrassment. I walked with flat feet and a limp. And I stood out.

I was lucky to have connections, friends and family who remembered me. People who loved me. Sue came to visit me. Sue and I met when we started university in 1990. Any time we had to do a group assignment, we tried to do it together. We thought alike and worked alike. We had similar values and we cared about each other.

Sue was a mature-age student with four children. She worked her heart out to get through the three years of university, and she passed everything with flying colours. She was, is, a woman of strength, courage, and faith. I have always been proud to call Sue my friend.

She came to visit me at Mt Wilga. With her, she brought a beautiful old-fashioned pink teacup with fuchsia roses on the inside and gold trim along the edges. It was made of fine china and had a lovely matching saucer. It was very elegant. She also gave me the most delicately scented little pyramid tea bags from a company in Singapore. They came in a long black box with antique gold details. It was such a thoughtful thing to bring.

Sue and I used to meet up at T2 Tea Rooms at Macquarie Centre when they sold tea and cake. We'd sit for hours, sipping tea from their fancy mismatched teapots, cups, and saucers. We'd laugh, complain, and chat about family, work, and the world. They closed that lovely place, probably because good friends like Sue and I sat for hours over one pot of tea and cost them a fortune!

Sue's rose teacup and saucer sat on my tray table at Wilga and was admired by all who came into the room. I shared the story of the gift and our friendship. Embarrassingly, the dinner ladies knew I didn't like their tea, but I was grateful for a cup of hot water in my fancy teacup so I could use my sweet-smelling tea bags. Those tea bags became famous throughout the corridors.

I worked with Lynette at Holy Cross. She was there the year before I was, when the whole school was made up of thirty-two children. It was the most wonderful place, with the most beautiful opportunities for the children in our care. We loved every child there, and we knew every one of them.

Lynette eventually moved to the US with her husband. She continued to work over there. They were very lucky because she was a gifted teacher. While I was a guest at Mt Wilga, Lynette returned to Australia because she missed her own children. She was only here for two weeks, but while she was here, she heard that I was not well. Lynette made time to come and see me.

I hadn't told many people from work about what had happened. At first, I thought it would get better. Then I was embarrassed. Then I kept thinking I would get better, for years I thought that. Maybe I was frightened another Deano Bonnello would emerge: *'Hey, Fat Mary Allen. Hey, Limpy Mary Allen.'* You just never knew.

But Lynette was different. She was my friend. She came to see me, and she saw how challenging things were. I kept a smile on my face, as I always did, and tried to be positive. It was hard to watch my friend walk out and know that I could not.

Carmen was another person I worked with at Holy Cross. Like Lynette, she was there before I was, and like Lynette, she came to visit me at Mt Wilga, she and her husband. I was so grateful for all the visits. I could see the surprise in people's faces when I had to get up to walk. I looked and sounded the same. But then, when it was time to move, I was a different person, almost like an old lady who wobbled and stumbled. I never made a creaking or complaining noise. I just got on with it and tried to move. But I could see the shock in people's faces that the movement wasn't right.

John, my brother, came to visit. His mode of transport surprised me. He came after work. I heard a strange squeaking coming down the corridor on the polished floor after dinner, almost like a squelching sound. Then John arrived in the doorway, with his pushbike!

'What on earth! Where did you come from?'

'Work.'

'But how did you get here?'

'I rode to Strathfield Station, caught the train to Hornsby, then rode from Hornsby to here.'

I had no idea about any of those distances, but it sounded like a mammoth trek, especially in the dark!

'I can't stay long,' he said, giving me a hug. It was great to see him. He hadn't seen me since before the 15th of July. I think he was surprised at how bad things were.

One day I had an appointment with Dr Leong. She always looked so beautiful with her stick-straight jet-black hair and her perfectly lipstick-stained red lips. She was wafer-thin in her red and black tight dress. Her sky-high patent black heels teased me, telling me they were able to tap tap tap on the floor while I had to clomp and plod and flop.

Her beautifully fitted-out feet both pointed in the same forward direction, while my clodhoppers pointed wherever they wanted, never in the same direction.

'What will happen if everything still hurts like this when it's time to go home?' I asked her.

'Usually people just get used to it.'

I just stared at her.

'You just have to get used to it.'

By this stage, the concrete boots were like lead. How would I ever get used to the heaviness and the heat and the daggers and the pain? I wondered how someone in her high-heeled shoes could say, *'Just get used to it.'* How could anyone who had never felt the hellish agony of Transverse Myelitis say that to someone living within it? *'Just get used to it.'*

'And what if I can't walk?'

'We'll teach you how to use a power chair.'

And we looked at each other, like we were in the middle of a staring competition in which she dared me to say something. My eyes started to burn. Dr Leong said goodbye and turned on her shiny black high heels, leaving me sitting on the edge of my Mt Wilga bed in the barbed wire body that I just had to get used to.

The staring competition was over. Dr Leong was gone.

Did that mean she had won?

Her tapping was getting softer down the hallway.

I was crying, a silent, heaving mess. Big, fat, heavy tears rolled down my cheeks as I took silent, sobbing breaths.

That's when Sandra came to the door. She was with her youngest daughter, Kate, both wearing big smiles. Sandra's face changed when she saw me. I was looking into a mirror of sadness.

'I just passed your mum and dad in the hallway. I'll go and get them.'

And she left me in my misery to fetch my parents. I could not believe I would be leaving Mt Wilga in pain and in a power chair.

Mum and Dad came in. I needed to see them. Sometimes you just need to see your mum and dad and you feel better. When they're gone, dead, the world is never the same. The balance is off, and it just never goes back.

Sandra followed when I'd calmed down. We've been friends since we were ten. We finished school together. I was one of Sandra's bridesmaids; she was one of mine. I'm one of her daughter's godmothers. She was there on the day my babies were born, she came into my room before Mum and Dad because she said she was my sister!

She was there throughout my marriage breakdown; she was with me when Mum and Dad died. She's been there like a warm blanket. Actually, she made me a warm blanket, it says, *'Friends forever, never apart, maybe in distance but never in heart.'* I know Sandra would do anything. When I was in Mt Wilga, she checked in on Mum and Dad for me when I couldn't. At Mum's funeral, when Mike's touch was so obviously absent, Sandra put her hand on me and said, 'You are the strongest person I know.'

I needed to hear that.

Mum and Dad only made it a few times to Mt Wilga before I got a phone call from Mum.

'Dad has to go in for a triple bypass.'

'What! When?'

'Tomorrow. He went for his stress test and Dr Jagger doesn't want him to go home.'

'Where will he have the operation?'

'Norwest.'

We didn't know how long he'd be in hospital, and Mum didn't know how she'd drive to see him. Her friend Maureen did lots of driving for her. People pull together, don't they? It was a real worry for everyone. Dad was seventy-five. His father died from heart issues at sixty-nine, so it was in the family. And he was under a lot of stress.

I called Mike, 'We have to go to Norwest. Now.'

All the older people at Mt Wilga seemed to enjoy their time there. They used their time to do their physio, OT, and exercise physiology, and to rest.

'Rest is as important as your exercise,' I was told.

But how could I keep still and rest when I knew I needed to get home? I knew that Mum and Dad were still travelling from Windsor to Lane Cove every weekday so Mike could continue going to work. My sisters, Catherine and Veronica and my friend Christine were helping Mike with Alex and Adelaide at the house. I was desperate to get home. Rest seemed like a waste of time. I know now that it isn't, but at the time, I just had to keep moving.

I watched the older people come into Mt Wilga, stay for a while, and then go home. Many of them talked about how their spouse at home had found them a new house to buy or rent for when they got back.

'There's no way I'm going home until our house is ready,' said one lady.

She needed a rail down the side of her house. I think she was in there with a knee problem. She just refused to go home until her husband installed a mega rail from the front of the house to the back. Other people organised whole new houses. I couldn't believe it.

Brian, the social worker, asked about our house. 'Are there any challenges that you can think of for when you go home?'

Oh my goodness! Where would I begin?

First, there were the steps, twenty-six from the car down to the house, crooked and winding, without any kind of rail. They were so bad that I got Alex and Adelaide into gymnastics when they were eighteen months old so they could learn how to fall. They were a death trap for anyone with a body that worked.

Every time I carried those baby capsules down, I concentrated so that I wouldn't drop them, and when I bounced the double pram up and down, it's a wonder the children didn't bounce out or end up with a brain injury. They were terrifying, a definite challenge.

Then there were the twenty-six steps that led from the house to the laundry underneath. The laundry was an important part of the house with little children, and those steps were another challenge. They also led to the backyard, where there was a trampoline and a climbing frame. We needed to be able to get there so Adelaide and Alex could play. The backyard was the only small flat part of land that we owned. It wasn't fair for them to be stuck in the house because of me. It was essential for me to be able to walk up and down steps.

There were two dogs in the backyard, a beagle named Mercedes and a beaglaire named Porsche. They made the back steps even more challenging. They ran up and down and got underfoot. They were Mike's pets. I was always so scared of dogs, terrified. I saw Mum get bitten once by a yappy terrier when I was very little, and I've never forgotten it.

At the front of the house, there were tiles, very slippery, uneven tiles that had years of grime from leaves, moisture, and mildew. When they were wet, they were like an ice-skating rink. You could almost stand at one end and slide to the front door. Another challenge, especially for someone who'd only walked on carefully maintained hospital floors for ages.

I had experience with the dangers of the house. Both before and after 2013. In 2018 we had a little friend of Alex and Adelaide's over to play. It was the Saturday of the Long Weekend in 2018.

'Just stop screaming! There's no one around.'

I almost whispered it, but by this stage I was angry.

'It's the long weekend, Mike. Everyone's away.'

I knew all the neighbours were away: the ones at 73 were at Old Bar, the ones at 77 were at Nowra, the ones across the road were in Newcastle. We were the only ones at home.

'Help!' he hollered again and again, over and over, in that ridiculous, raucous panic. How dare he be the one to panic? He wasn't the one lying on the ground.

'Somebody! Help!'

As usual, it was all about him. That was his favourite line, 'It's all about me.'

All I needed was for him to shut his mouth and help me get up off the ground. This was one time it could be about me. By now, my head was starting to feel really hot and sticky.

Was it sweat? It shouldn't have been, it was July. I didn't want the children to see me. They were only six.

I still had the plate in my hand. The chops had fallen off and landed next to me in the dirt on the pavers. How would I explain to Adelaide's friend's mum that I'd fallen? I always tried to pretend there was nothing wrong with me. That I was normal - if there is such a thing. She wouldn't let her come for another playdate, that's for sure. Mike must have locked the girls inside. As usual, he didn't worry about Alex. Little Alex, only six as well.

'Mum.' His big chocolate eyes were calm. Smooth, still discs. His voice was smooth, unlike the wailing that enveloped us from above. 'I think you're bleeding.'

I felt the pool of hot stickiness around my head. I finally let go of the plate.

'Call an ambulance, Mike. Stop screaming.'

I could hear the lady on the other end of the 000 call, and from my position on the ground, I had to answer her questions.

'Yes, I'm breathing.'

And I could put my four fingers in the hole straight through to my skull.

'No, I haven't passed out. Yes, I'm still bleeding. No, I haven't moved. Stop swearing at her, Mike.'

I needed a towel.

Alex's calm brown eyes came into focus again.

'Do you think you need an ice pack?'

'Alex, I think that would be a great idea.'

And before the towel arrived,

before the ambulance arrived,

but while the screaming was getting worse,

I was gifted a zip-lock mini snack bag filled with ice cubes and an almost imperceptible,

'I love you, Mum.'

Then the paramedics arrived. There was a heated discussion with Mike about how to make the trip with me up the stairs, those rotten stairs, the new, improved 'safety stairs' (this was after I got home from Mt Wilga). So, with the ice pack tucked in the hole in my head, I flung the towel off in a very dramatic gesture and said in an extremely assertive voice - especially considering I was laying on the ground at the time, 'Get out of my way and let me walk up the stairs!'

'Ooh, you've got a tough one here,' said the ambulance guy, thinking he was being funny.

In a trail of blood and clomping feet, still holding the zip-lock bag of ice, through gritted teeth I said, 'You have no idea,' and left them all in my wake. I waited in the ambulance for them all to get their acts together and join me.

Another challenge was inside the house. There was very limited space, filled with lots of two-year-olds' paraphernalia, trip hazards galore. This wouldn't generally be a bad thing, but for a person prone to falls, it was not good.

The house itself had two bedrooms. The kitchen was the size of a shoebox, size five. The bathroom tiles were falling off the original 1950s walls into the original 1950s bath and onto the original 1950s floors. The original 50s shower head leaked, and the floor and shower curtain were always wet.

I was always looking for an alternative place to live. realestate.com was my favourite webpage. I was on a first-name basis with the local real estate agents, many of them knew me.

I was looking for somewhere Alex and Adelaide would have space. Somewhere the kitchen was practical and the bathroom was safe. It didn't have to be a fancy house or a big house. I just wanted a small, easy-to-live-in home with three bedrooms. If it was flat enough for Mum and Dad to come and visit comfortably, that would be a bonus.

I knew Mike liked Lane Cove because his best friend lived in Johnston Crescent, where we were. I liked Lane Cove too, it was close to the city, close to the bush, close to shops and schools, and not too far from family. But I did not like the house. It was too small and downright dangerous.

So when I was asked, 'Can you think of any challenges at home?' I could think of quite a few. But because I wanted to go home, I minimised them. And I made it my mission to overcome them.

The OT said she'd pay a visit to our house to assess the risks and see if it would be safe for me to leave Mt Wilga. I was excited because I was going too. It was organised for Tuesday.

Mike had organised Les, his builder friend, to be there. Mike's mother was there too, she'd been staying with him for a few days. I still couldn't believe she told my mum she thought it would be best for Alex and Adelaide to move to Northern NSW with her. No consultation with me, their mother! If that had happened, I would have moved heaven and earth to get there. Maybe I would have taken one of those power chairs and driven it along the Pacific Highway!

Mum and Dad were going to be there. Mike's sister-in-law also wanted to come because apparently she'd been visiting on Tuesdays. A lot had been going on in that house, and with my children, that I didn't know about.

I knew it would be too overwhelming for Alex and Adelaide to have that many extra people all at once: Mike and I, Mum and Dad, Mike's mother Barbara, Mike's sister-in-law Lorraine, the nanny, Sharon the OT, Mike's friend the builder, and Brian the social worker, all in a two-bedroom house.

It was the first time I'd been home in three months, and I wasn't able to stay, it was just for the afternoon.

I called Lorraine.

'Thank you for supporting Mike. I'm just thinking about all the people that are going to be at the house next week. I think it'll be too much for the children. Would you mind not coming that day?'

Sbe agreed.

It was all sorted. Or so I thought.

'How dare you try to cut me off from my supports!' came Mike, bellowing down the phone as I sat on my bed all alone in my room at Mt Wilga.

Mike was headed home to the nanny, his mother, his sister-in-law, his best friend the next-door neighbour, and our children.

'Do not ever speak to me like that again,' I was calm.

After that, my rings were locked in the top drawer of the bedside table to make sure they were safe. Just in case.

The rings stayed in the top drawer.

Mike didn't notice the missing rings. Mum did.

The day with all those people and their tape measures was huge.

I stood at the top of those deadly steps, even more deadly now than ever before. I looked down, and there, framed in the lounge room window, better than any masterpiece, bouncing up and down were my babies! Holding onto the back of the lounge and screaming with delight as they bounced as though on the trampoline we'd paid thousands for.

They were all I could see! We could've saved a fortune on the trampoline with the 'wonderful safety features' and just said, 'Here you go, look out the window and jump on the lounge!' I'm sure they would've had just as much fun!

Someone put the fabric belt with the yellow handles on me and started pulling at me as I headed off down the steps. Mum and Dad were there, off to the side. There were so many people, the nanny and Mike's mum were inside the house; his sister-in-law didn't come. Mike and the builder were with Brian. Sharon was trying to hold on to me. She's probably the one who put the belt on me.

That's when the friendly next-door neighbour popped out to see what was going on. 'You really can't imagine how hard it has been for Mike, having a disabled wife.'

I couldn't believe what I was hearing come out of her mouth. I took my very strong right hand, motioned up and down my body and said to her, 'This... this is the disabled wife.'

And the disabled wife left her standing there to tend to more important things.

The upshot was that, surprise, surprise, the house wasn't safe for me to go home. They wouldn't let me leave Mt Wilga until changes had been made.

'There need to be steps at the front, grab rails at the front, steps at the back, grab rails at the back, a safety rail all the way round in the shower, a safety rail on at least one side in the toilet, non-slip tiles on the bathroom floor, tiles on the wall in the shower recess where the old ones had fallen off, a new shower head that didn't leak, a hand-held shower head, something to be done about the turning circle in the living space to fit a wheelchair, improvements to the access in the kitchen.' There was so much that needed to be done.

Mike said it would take a long time and cost a lot of money.

Sharon said, 'If it's too much, you could do all the works except the back steps and put them off until a later time. If you say you'll get them done, you can go home and get them done later.'

That was never going to happen.

The front steps were done: concrete was poured over the top of one third of the old steps, and timber replaced the bottom two thirds. The front rail was replaced. It took a long time because there was a rather severe bend.

'You could get home quicker if you didn't need the whole thing. That's what's taking the time,' Mike told me. 'We could just do a straight rail at the top section then a straight rail at the bottom section and just leave the bend in the middle out.'

'That bend is probably the most dangerous part,' I told him. 'The whole idea is to be safe.'

The shower and toilet rails, the non-slip tiles and the shower head were all done. But the back steps were not. They were never done. To this day, they still haven't been done. The kitchen was never changed, the turning circle was never enlarged, the bathroom never ended up with tiles on the walls. And there were always so many trip hazards. There was just nowhere to put anything.

There was talk about a wheelchair and a walker. Anyway, how would we get them down the stairs? And there was no point, because where would anything like that fit? My turning circles were so clunky, I didn't know how I was going to fit. I'd been away from home for so long that I didn't know if I would fit.

Me, or my rings that were locked in the top drawer of the bedside table at Mt Wilga.

We should have moved.

Mt Wilga was a rehabilitation facility. People went there to rehabilitate, to get better. I discovered that 'getting better' does not always mean getting back to the way you were before. It has taken me a long time to accept that. For a long time, I would wake up in the morning and lie in bed thinking, Today's the day! Today's the day that I will be fixed!

Today's the day that I will be back to normal. Today's the day that I won't have to worry about wetting myself or having an accident or passing wind at the wrong time. Today's the day that I'll be able to run in the park again with Alex and Adelaide. Today's the day!

But it was never the day.

My body never got better.

The pain never improved.

The muscle cramps never stopped.

The fatigue never went away.

People would offer very unhelpful comparisons.

'It's like that time I got chicken pox,' I was told.

'It's like when I had that toothache,' someone else offered.

'My sister's husband's mother's next-door neighbour's cousin's friend got the flu once. It's the same as that.'

'I think it happened to bring your relationship closer to God.'

Really?

It's not the chicken pox.

It's nothing to do with my teeth.

Or a flu.

My relationship with God was fine, thanks. Not that it was really anyone's business but mine and God's. TM is none of those things, nor is it like any of those things.

When I came home, one person very close to us greeted me with, 'So what can't you do?'

Really? That was the first thing he said to me. 'So, what can't you do?' What a ridiculous thing to say.

I had to shake my head. I smiled at him, and in a split second, so many thoughts and feelings burned through my mind: thoughts of all those school reports I had written and how we always identify what a child can do, never what they cannot do. Then, what a nasty thing to say, why point out what I'm not capable of? And still in the same flash of thought came the idea that this question showed how ignorant he was of everything I had been through. How stupid for a grown adult.

'Well, I can't run a marathon, but I never could, so it really doesn't matter, does it?'

'You don't need to be so rude,' he said.

Really? That was his response. That I was being rude to him. I turned and walked away.

By this stage, I knew Prof Herkes too well to call him "Prof Herkes." He was Dr Herkes. He wasn't a professor locked away in a university. He was a doctor who had saved my life.

Dr Herkes said to me, 'It would be easier to say you got hit by a bus. People would understand that.' He was right. It has always been challenging to explain Transverse Myelitis to people, especially at the start. But people who know me and love me listen and watch and see what it has done to my body, to my mind, and to my life.

Transverse Myelitis has stolen a lot. It stole my ability to move and to feel and to look like I used to. It stole my ability to have the career that I loved. Sadly, it stole relationships.

On the flip side, it meant that I was at home with my children as they were growing up. I fought for that. It was not a popular decision, but it was the only decision. It was right for my children, and it was right for me. It has taken a long time, but I have started to find my voice again.

When I was in that Acute Stroke Ward, Ward 7F at Royal North Shore, I promised myself that I would speak for my voiceless inmates. Although our experiences were all different, we had our loss of self in common. It has taken me a long time, but this is it. Most of those roommates from 7F are probably gone now, but they would have been replaced very quickly. Probably straight away.

Shopping Expedition

There was a jewellery store in Lane Cove. It's still there: Stedman's Fine Jewellery. Its name sounds very impressive and suggests an imposing place with Roman-inspired columns and massive door handles, perhaps even a buzzer you need to press to be let in. It conjures the image of a shop filled with snobbish staff drifting about, pretending to be busy, hoping not to catch your eye so you think they're too important to serve the everyday person.

Instead, it's a tiny shopfront, about four metres wide, tucked down a side alley. Those four metres sparkle and shine, glisten and glow. The jewels whisper with the promise of a world that is beautiful and special, and as you walk past, they call to you, inviting you to look, to imagine what it's like to wear the handmade pieces on display. Sometimes there are diamonds, sometimes rubies or emeralds. Oh my goodness, the greens! And sometimes there are pearls, locked away in a glass cabinet.

Those cheeky pearls called to me. Like the song from Rodgers and Hammerstein's South Pacific, Bali Ha'i:

'Bali Ha'i may call you,

Any night, any day,

In your heart, you'll hear it call you: come away ... come away.'

They were giants. Those pearls.

'Bali Ha'i will whisper, 'Come to me! Come to me!'"

You could picture Bloody Mary standing on the sand, calling with her hands, wearing those beads and singing that sultry song, the palms waving in the breeze, the salt air on your face. The smoothest, largest, glossiest pearls my eyes have ever spied. With the sounds of the musical wafting in the background and temptation tapping me on the shoulder:

'Your own special hopes,

Your own special dreams,

Bloom on the hillside

And shine in the streams.

If you try, you'll find me

Where the sky meets the sea.

Here am I your special island

'Come to me, come to me," sang Bloody Mary on that beach in front of the gentle waves.'

'Just try me on. Feel me on your skin.' They were so warm and soft, almost still wet from the ocean. Each one was the size of a medium marble, sitting flush against my skin. They weren't bright white; they were a creamy colour that complemented my skin tone, and there were even some pinkish beauties in the mix. Oh, that string was irresistible.

But I resisted. I had to be strong. 'I will be 50 in a few years. I'll tell Mike about you, you thing of beauty – for when I turn 50!'

Mike resisted them. I never got those pearls. When he said to me, 'That will be the last jewellery you ever get,' when Alex and Adelaide were one, I thought he was joking.

He wasn't.

As I said, being at Mt Wilga was not like being in a hospital to be sick; it was being in a place to get better. They worked us really hard. Well, some people worked hard, others treated it more like a holiday. And that was entirely understandable. We were all there for different reasons: replacements, strokes, operations, accidents, illnesses. They gave us so many opportunities to get well.

One day they put me in a minibus, one of those 15-seater types, and drove me to the enormous Westfield at Hornsby. At first, when I was getting ready to go, I didn't think much of it. I went shopping all the time; I took Adelaide and Alex all the time. We used to go shopping or to a café, and I didn't think anything of it.

On this particular day, it was a very different experience. I had graduated to a wheelie walker by this stage, like the ones you see older people hunched over, pushing along. Mine was burgundy red. I hated it. I wasn't allowed to go anywhere without it. I was only allowed to walk the Wilga corridors with the walker. But you should have seen me go! They do say red goes faster!

'Do I really have to take the walker?'

'Yes. It will be safer if you have it with you.'

'I really don't want it.'

But I did as I was told, walked my wheels to the bus, handed them to the driver, and got in. The driver packed my wheels.

I couldn't believe how close we were to Westfield. We felt so far away from everything. There was a lurching excitement in the pit of my stomach, which was silly. I was only going to the shopping centre. The car park was dark. The bus stopped in a special spot that seemed designed to make it difficult for people who couldn't walk. Because I couldn't see my lower half, I really had no idea what it was doing. It had a mind and laws of its own.

'Is this some kind of test or something?'

'Will you be alright on your own? Or would you like someone to come with you?'

'I'll be okay.' I was pleased at the thought of having time on my own.

'If you need to change floors, use the lift, not the escalators. We'll meet back here in 45 minutes. Okay?'

'Okay. See you then.'

I was off with confidence as the words were trailing out of my mouth. It was the first taste of freedom I had had since

15 July. I had 45 minutes, and I was not going to waste a millisecond of it!

The confidence soon waned. I started to feel like I was in one of the displays in Stedman's Fine Jewellery. I felt very tiny, surrounded by a lot of very loud, very sparkly things. Unlike Stedman's, these sparkles didn't call invitingly; they were garish and gaudy, like a disco ball. There were shards of bright light jarring at me from every angle: above, below, beside, even inside. There were bolts of noise coming at me in the shape of announcements, music, shouting, and screaming. With every new noise, I felt my innards scream.

There were smells so overpowering I thought I would vomit: perfume counters where the scent filled my nostrils and stuck to the fine hairs in my nose; food smells that were greasy, burnt, and disgusting. I held so tightly onto my wheelie walker that my knuckles went the same white colour as the intense tiles on the ground. Forty-five minutes was going to be a lot longer than I thought. It was sensory overload.

I was pleased to have the wheels. Weaving in and out of the crowd was frightening.

'Can't you see you're going to knock me over? Charlie! Get out of my way!' So many Charlies. I decided I needed a yellow wheelie walker with a big scoop on the front. And a hard hat. And a high-vis vest. That way I could go like a bulldozer: put my head down and just power on! Maybe even a flashing light would help. Although, the way some people looked at me, I am sure they thought, Ooh, I can beat her, and they just put their foot down and tried to race me. Some people have no idea how to be around other people, let alone people with a disability. Not that I knew to use that word about myself. Especially someone locked inside Stedman's Fine Jewellery with sights, sounds, and smells shooting at them from every direction.

Like I said: sensory overload.

I was back at our rendezvous just inside the 45 minutes. Any longer than that would have been way too long. It was a relief to see my teammates with their walkers and be able to make our way back to the bus. The dark car park felt safe after the overwhelm of Westfield. The drive back to Mt Wilga blurred in my memory, and I slept when I got back. It was a lot. My confidence had been shaken, but not broken.

Driver's Licence

When I was doing my HSC, I had a timetable that meant all my subjects were squeezed together over one week, then a week's break before I had Ancient History. In that time of nothing, which could have been a bonus or an unfortunate switch-off period, I turned 18. Lots of the other students were talking about getting their driver's licence and actually getting it. They were so excited about it. I just wanted to get through the exams. My strategy was to ignore Ancient History, study for everything else, and when I had finished, devote that week completely to Pompey and Augustus.

That turned out to be a good strategy. My friends of the Ancient World carried me down the Appian Way to glory, and we celebrated in a fine way through the gates of Rome the following January when the postie delivered my results. It paid off to ignore my Grecian and Roman friends, and not to think about my driver's licence.

At that stage of our lives, everyone was excited about when and how they would get their licence. The streets around our school were lined with mum and dad's dad cars, plastered with P Plates dangling from the front and back. I wasn't really interested.

Until after the exams. Then I traded Caesar's chariots and his four horses in my study for study about four wheels. I could concentrate on the next phase. I didn't think I was too excited about getting my driver's licence, but it was the next thing in life, so I studied hard. Dad took me for my first driving lesson in the Kombi on Fairey Road. That was his go-to driving-instructing place for all of us. It was fairly straight and relatively deserted. The main things we had to dodge were potholes after the rain. All seven of us learnt to drive on Fairey Road.

'Right, kids, who wants to come? Mary Anne's going to drive the car.'

A little bit of privacy would have been nice. Mum and John were the only ones who stayed home. There was a Kombi with Dad and me and five younger siblings, all as excited as the family's first learner driver!

It was the Saturday after my last exam. Dad drove to the top of Fairey Road where the gates to the sewerage treatment plant were locked. There was a slight incline. There was electricity in the air. Dad reversed the car and switched it off.

He got out of the driver's seat. I got out of the passenger seat. The chatter in the car turned to whispers.

Dad walked to the front of the car and put the cardboard L on the number plate. I walked to the back of the car and did the same. The whispers in the car turned to a buzz.

Dad got in the passenger seat. For the first time, I got in the driver's seat. My head pounded in my ears. The buzz in the car turned to absolute silence. All passengers sat bolt upright and stared straight ahead. Dad was the calmest of all of us.

Check your mirrors. Top. Sides. Adjust. Check the steering wheel. Adjust. Seatbelts on. Foot on the brake. Turn the key. Last check in the mirror. Check over the shoulder. 'You can take your foot off the brake.'

Was I ready? I knew how to change a tyre. Dad wouldn't let any of us drive until we could show him that we could change a tyre, change the oil, and water. But it hit me that I had control of this great big machine with all these people I loved sitting inside. It was a big responsibility.

'Slowly take your foot off the brake. Ok, that's good. Maybe a bit faster.'

I started to release the brake, and we rolled down Fairey Road. I wasn't really driving; we were just rolling. That didn't matter, none of the others knew that. We were moving. It was a lot harder and a lot scarier than it looked when Mum and Dad drove. They made it look so effortless. Eventually the decline ran out, and I had to put my foot on the accelerator. Just like eventually I had to leave Fairey Road and join the big, wide road world.

'What do you mean I need to do a driving test?'

I didn't know, and no one told me until it got closer to the end of my time at Mt Wilga.

'Everyone who has a spinal cord injury or a brain injury has to do a driving test before they can have their driver's licence back again.'

'What do you mean 'back again'?'

'Your driver's licence has been cancelled.'

'So I can't drive?'

'Effectively. That's right.'

It was the OT, but not Sharon, who got to break the news to me. I hadn't even thought about losing my driver's licence. I just assumed that if I could walk, everything else I used to be able to do, like drive, would go along with it. It didn't cross my mind that someone would say to me, 'Hey, you can't drive!'

This was another hurdle that was put in front of me. 'What do I have to do to get my licence back? I need my licence. I need to be able to drive.'

Brian, the Return-to-Home person, explained it to me. 'You need to do a test. First a cognitive test to show that you are mentally okay to drive. You do that with the OT from Wilga. Then you do a driving test. You do that with an RTA driving examiner, but you can have a Wilga OT in the car with you, if you like.'

'Will it be in my car?'

'No. It will be in an RTA examiner's car so it has the dual controls.'

'Where will it be?'

'It's usually around Hornsby because they come and pick you up here at the front door.'

'But I don't know Hornsby. At all.'

'It will be like doing your Ls again.'

'No. It won't. I knew the area very well. And I knew my body.'

It was nothing like doing the Ls again. The stakes were much higher. Everyone who did their driver's licence exam expected to fail it at least once. But then most of us didn't. We expected to, but didn't.

Getting that driver's licence gave me so much independence. I had never dreamed how much I would love it. Had I known what it would have been like, Pompey and Augustus would have had a run for their money!

Losing My Independence

Losing my independence now didn't just mean losing independence for me; it meant losing the ability to get my babies around. It meant losing independence for my whole family. Getting my driver's licence this time meant so much more.

"Right, what is your full name?

The date?

Your birthday?

The Prime Minister?"

Again with the Prime Minister! Who was it this time? It was Kevin Rudd, Labor Party, Prime Minister number two of three that year, sandwiched between Julia Gillard – Labor – Australia's only woman PM, who was berated for her dress sense of all things, and Tony Abbott – Liberal. You really couldn't determine a person's mental acuity based on whether they knew who the Prime Minister was in 2013!

"Why are you here today?

How long have you held a driver's licence?"

"I'm doing my driving test.

Because I need to be able to get around.

My family needs my independence."

These questions were followed by about an hour and a half of questions about road rules. Instead of doing the test online, I did a spoken test, one-on-one with the driving OT from Mt Wilga. When I passed that part of the test, it was time to do the driving.

The Roads and Traffic Authority lady's car was parked in the front car park. It had dual controls so that if I didn't brake at the right time, she could press the pedal and stop the car. I was very nervous. After all, I had only been driving for 24 years, minus three months! I was going to do everything to the letter. I circled the car and checked the tyres. I got in, put my seat belt on, started the car, checked the rear-view mirror, checked the side mirrors. I thought about Fairey Road and let the car gently roll. I thought about Dad sitting next to me. We slowly crunched out of the car park and onto the roads of Hornsby.

'At the next intersection, you will turn left.' The indicators went on, I slowed down, and we turned left into the busier two lanes.

'At the traffic lights, please turn right.' I checked over my shoulder, checked the side mirror, indicated right, moved into the right lane, waited at the lights for the green arrow, and went when I could.

'At the roundabout, exit at the second exit.' Which really just meant go straight ahead. There were left turns, right turns, roundabouts, stop signs, give ways, pedestrian crossings, school zones, 60 zones, 80 zones, lane changes, you name it, we found it. I was the perfect driver. I knew I did everything right. But it was exhausting because I had not driven for three months, gosh, I had only just learned how to walk, and I was in unfamiliar territory.

'Go and take a seat,' the driving lady said to me.

'I'll be with you in a few minutes,' the Mt Wilga OT said.

And they left me in a little room. Surely they could have just said, 'Congratulations! You've passed,' instead of telling me to wait? Minutes always feel longer when you have to wait. I decided that I would speak up if I didn't get it. There shouldn't be any reason. I was a perfect driver.

'Mary Anne. Congratulations. You've passed,' the Wilga OT came and said. I never saw the RTA lady again.

Even though I had a spinal cord injury, I was allowed to drive. What a relief! Getting that driver's licence the second time meant more to me than getting it the first time. There was more at stake. I knew what I was missing out on if I didn't get it.

Residuals

'And the winner is ... Syd-en-ee, Australia.'

So many Australians were waiting for that announcement coming from Juan Carlos Samaranch in 1993. It came in the early hours of the morning. I was one of the few who slept through it.

In the lead-up to the 2000 Olympics, Sydney changed. Infrastructure increased and improved, people trained to take on volunteer roles, and we learnt about all sorts of sports that we'd never heard of, like Greco-Roman wrestling. What on earth was that? As a teacher, I was lucky; I had access to information to teach my students, so I got to learn along the way.

There was talk about all the crowds that would be coming into Sydney. All the people that would be coming in, but not going out, would mean we should be able to access cheaper overseas flights.

I grabbed that opportunity with both hands and ran with it like it was an Olympic sport! As soon as I could, I booked myself on a return flight and a 17-day 'UK and Ireland' Trafalgar bus trip. When the world counted down to Syd-en-ee, I counted down to Trafalgar! I couldn't wait.

Travel time was September. 'It will be perfect over there. Autumn,' everyone said. The only time I'd been to Europe was winter. It was amazing, so beautiful, with sparkling

Christmas lights, but I was looking forward to seeing things differently, green, with the fountains working.

As it got closer, I prepared: clothes, toiletries, tickets, everything. I have to admit, though, as the atmosphere built, I felt a twinge of anti-Olympic-ness. Even anti-patriotism. How could I leave when the biggest cultural event in my living memory was going to happen? The world would be watching us, and I was leaving.

As expected, Sydney sparkled. I showed my support by watching at night from the other side of the world. I had a wonderful time on my bus tour: buying lace and crystal in Waterford, kissing the Blarney Stone and hoping I didn't share germs with the thousands of others who also hung upside down through a little stone window to do the same (I wonder if the locals would ever do such a thing?). Climbing narrow, winding staircases in castles so old they were feats of engineering to be made without modern tools. I wandered through the Tower of London and stayed well clear of the vicious but beautiful horses at Buckingham Palace. I gazed at the lochs, in the hope that maybe I would be the one to discover Nessie.

And when I arrived in Ireland, I had an overwhelming sense of coming home. I had to gulp the tears that welled as I thought, I am home. It was my first time there, but it felt like coming home.

I got back into Sydney just before the Closing Ceremony. Sydney was being praised and patting herself on the back for holding the best-ever Olympics: best organised, best volunteers, most welcoming, just the best of everything. It's funny; whoever holds the Olympics seems to have 'the best.' But of course, the Sydney Games were the best.

Schools all went back, and life returned to a sort of normal for the world's best city after the Closing on 1 October. Things were not quite over. An army of workers moved in to get things ready for the 2000 Paralympic Games. So before we, as a city, could fall into a slump, miserable that the best time of our lives was over, we prepared for the next party. The Paralympic Games were not new; ours was the XI Summer Paralympic Games. But it never got anywhere near the airplay that the Olympic Games got. Sydney was going to change that. We just had no idea how much.

The organisers' idea was to make sure the athletes had as much support as possible. They wanted to fill the stadium, crowd out the concourse, raise the roof off every indoor arena. They wanted every athlete of every ability to know they were being encouraged and that they were welcome. And they wanted to educate people who weren't part of the Paralympic world. Some very clever conversations must have been had around how to do all of this, because the organisers decided that the best way to achieve all those things was to get schools involved. Where else could they find tens of thousands of people already in a learning environment, with teachers right there ready to go? By the time 18 October 2000 came along, the students of our schools knew our Paralympic team, they knew the sports, and most importantly, they all had access to tickets!

We didn't have to go into a ballot or a draw to get tickets to the Paralympics. Children's tickets were $10, adults cost $15. And those tickets took you to whichever event you wanted to go to all day. Special school-only trains ran throughout the rail system to Olympic Park. Everything was done to encourage schools to go along and support the athletes.

The school where I worked was a brand-new school. In 2000, we had only kindergarten, Years 1, 2, and 3. Bright and early, all the students and teachers met at Blacktown Station. We were assigned a carriage number on the special train, and off we went. If the train could have been propelled by excitement, we would have got there in record time! The coming together of so many children was unprecedented and incredible.

The biff and blood-curdling boof of the wheelchair basketball was very popular. So was wheelchair rugby, but then I guess when you're coming from the world of the playground where British Bulldog is banned, anyone who plays 'Murderball' reaches superhero status!

The track and field events were amazing too. The amputee runners with blades instead of legs ran so gracefully. How did they feel wearing those blades? They made their movements look so smooth. They sort of bounded along the track, making themselves taller than the regular height of a person. They looked like they could 'leap tall buildings in a single bound.' I wondered if that was how it felt. Did it feel as beautiful to go through the air as it looked? Or was it more sinister? Did the blade rub on the skin? Did it make you feel sick to bounce like that when we're technically not made that way? Do you feel like you're always on a trampoline? And what happens when you take them off? Do you feel heavy, like when you get out of a pool?

'The research suggests that one third of people with Transverse Myelitis will get better. One third will improve and be left with residuals. The final third will not show any improvement past the initial onset.'

'What do you mean by residuals?'

'Well, that could mean anything from muscle aches to nerve pain. Residuals could mean paralysis.'

To me, the advice was not greatly encouraging. I didn't like the sound of those last two options. Residuals was a nice way of saying, 'you'll have a lot to deal with.' I decided I was going to be in the first third that was going to fully recover. Like I had a choice.

'I think I can feel something!' Brian, the social worker, was the first person I told. It was the tiniest twinge at first, just behind my right knee. I thought the slicing feeling was a good sign, an indication of improvement and a cause for celebration, like the big toe that moved in the very early days.

'Surely that must be a good sign? It feels a bit like I'm wearing a long sock with really tight fishing wire around the top, and it gets tighter and tighter every time I move.'

It wasn't pleasant. It was the opposite, actually, slicing into my leg but leaving no signs. It was a feeling where there hadn't been anything. A residual, perhaps? Pushing me into that middle third?

I kept walking and bending my legs and lifting those pegs. I had chats with Rob as he 'just happened to be walking by.' And at night, I eventually showered by myself and settled down to watch Dannii Minogue host Australian Idol. I loved to see what she was wearing more than the singing. The days felt long and exhausting.

The fishing wire tied around my left leg too. And it tightened to the point I thought my calf muscles would detach. They didn't. Instead, the feeling moved south towards my feet. Now I was lugging around heavy concrete boots, like those knee-high socks but made of concrete. They constricted with my walking, and their insides grew a lining made of molten rusty nails and jagged barbed wire. The boots kept my feet flat, and the concrete made them drag. I burned and bled on the inside of those boots, but again, no marks or signs appeared to show the pain.

Torture? Or residuals?

All I wanted was to get home. So I walked and worked and practised and stumbled. I never fell. There were rails, smooth, shiny wooden rails, everywhere to grab onto to prevent the falls. And as I walked and worked, those residuals got worse: the concrete tightened, the fishing line constricted, the metal burned, and the barbs stabbed.

And this is what I 'just had to get used to.' Honestly, the thought crossed my mind: how will I ever live with this medieval torture device?

By the time I left Mt Wilga, calf muscles were so tight that it felt like they were wound up like springs. Each step, although I couldn't feel my legs, only the residuals, felt like I had the blades of those Paralympians ready to spring me through the air, boots and all. The difference was that I was clunky, and my steps looked flat, not fluid like the athletes'.

I developed a pain just under and behind my left shoulder blade. It was a dagger, slicing through the layers of skin, muscle, and fat, almost to the left breast. This dagger was razor-sharp and pointy at the tip. I felt the slicing motion as it went in and out, shearing forwards and back. No blood was drawn. The dagger was my own body, the messages trying to get through a damaged spinal cord.

The inside of the left arm burnt with the feeling of excessive ice. Patches were completely numb, and others were in a constant ice-fire. And I was still wearing those nappies.

'They're not nappies,' I was constantly told.

'Well, what would you call them?'

'We call them pads.' But they didn't look like any pads I'd ever seen. They were a grown-up version of the pull-up pants that toddlers and babies wore. The only difference was that these didn't have Disney pictures drawn on them.

I was driving the Kombi to visit my friend. Mary and Col had just come back from their honeymoon. I was bridesmaid. The Kombi didn't have air conditioning (it was a 1974 model; I don't know if air conditioning in cars was even invented when it came off the production line!), so the front windows were down to let the air in. It was a sweltering day, one of those Sydney summer days when the cicadas were deafening and the magpies even wandered around with their beaks open to cool off.

The steering wheel was like a truck. There was no power steering. And the view was great because you sat up high in the driver's seat.

Something touched my arm, between the wrist and the elbow. Just lightly. I was sure it must have been a fly, so I shooed it away. Still, the lightest feathery touch on my arm moved. Another shoo. It still moved. Now it was on my elbow. This time, as I shooed it, I looked down to see what I was shooing.

The biggest, hairiest huntsman spider I had ever seen! Crawling on me! It was so enormous, its hirsute legs wrapped from one side of my arm right around to the other, a bangle made of spideriness! This time I didn't shoo; I walloped!

I could feel ants and spiders crawling up and down my body, from my shoulder to my ankles. There were none on my feet, and if there were, I couldn't feel them. They were drowned out by the noise of all the other residuals. Up and down they went, their touch lighter near my ankles and heavier near the dagger. I could feel them inside those new boots.

Messages were getting through alright, just not the right ones.

If the lesions on my spine were like a car crash, then the messages to and from the brain were the car finding a new route. I imagine most of us start out with a nice smooth ride that we don't even feel. A sports car. An electric sports car that makes no sound and stops to rest at the lights. We start off on a perfectly smooth road, fast and efficient. An autobahn. I was lucky. That's what mine had been for 42 years.

Now my spinal cord was off-road. Those messages had to navigate cliffs and crevices, potholes where bits got missed, and pools of mud where some got stuck. And the sleek and silent sports car that carried the messages was no more. It was a weathered old 1971 (same model as me) Datsun 1200. A Paddy Basher!

The Big Long Sigh

'What do you mean Adelaide is naughty?'

'Well, any time we pack up, she pulls everything back out of the drawer.'

'I don't understand. That doesn't sound like Adelaide at all. She likes everything to be organised. She knows where everything belongs and where it has to go.'

We always made setting up and packing away part of our games and activities, so Adelaide and Alex knew that whatever they got out had to go away in the same place from where it came: scissors in the scissor tray, textas in the texta tray, paper and glue in the paper and glue tray, wooden train set under the red craft table, cushions in the tent, books on the bookshelf, plates and cups in the sink. Everything had a proper place. And even as two-year-olds, Adelaide and Alex knew that if they got something out, they were responsible for putting it back in the same place, in the same condition.

It bothered me that while I was encaged somewhere, learning how to walk, my babies were imprisoned at home, being kept away from Mummy, not allowed to talk to or about her, doing who knows what and being told they were naughty.

Please don't tell my two-year-olds that they are naughty. Especially when they are in the midst of a family trauma.

I knew my children, and I knew they weren't naughty. I said to my Mum, 'What two-year-old makes a decision to be naughty?'

None.

'We were reading this book, just before bedtime,' I can't remember who the helper was.

'That's great, thank you for keeping their schedule going as usual.'

'We were on the lounge in their room.' Well, so far, everything sounded as it should.

'Alex and Adelaide were in their pyjamas, ready for bed. They were in their sleeping bags.' They had these funny sleeping bags that were simply a sack with a head hole, two arm holes, and a great long zipper down the front. The winter sleeping bags were nice and warm, and the summer sleeping bags were a calico-weight fabric. They were very roomy and took away the need for blankets, which was great when you had someone like Adelaide, who did gymnastics in the middle of the night and ended up all over the cot.

So far, it all sounded fine. 'We'd show them a book, but they'd never want the one we chose. They wanted to choose their own.'

'That's what they normally do. They choose a book each, and I choose one. Unless they're too long.' Still, I couldn't see how that was naughty.

'Well, they both keep wanting the same book.'

'Oh. That's lucky! Only one book!'

'Yes. They both want Rudie Nudie.' They used to love this book so much. We all used to love it so much! It was so much fun to read together.

When we got to the bit that said, *Rudie Nudie hugged up in a bundle,* and there was a picture of a mum kneeling on the bathroom floor wiping two wet nudie children, we had a giant Adelaide, Alex, and Mummy cuddle. A great big squeezy, wobbly one. Every time we read that part, we had to do it.

And then came the riotous part! Dressed in their sleeping bags, they knew what was coming. Alex and Adelaide knew every line of the book because we had read it so many times. We were surrounded by books. They loved books and reading and writing and drawing. We got to their favourite part:

Rudie Nudie out the door!

And they were off! They sprang off the lounge in their sleeping bags like rabbits released before a dog race. Four little feet in four little corners of two little sleeping bags. Stretched to the max. Racing out the door like penguins while I shouted the next line after them:

Rudie Nudie on the floorboards!

Off like waddling rockets! Where were they going? Nowhere, really. Out the door, into the hallway, around the corner, into the lounge room, past the dining table, into the hallway, and back to their room for

Rudie Nudie on the rug,

to dive onto the lounge for another cuddle before

Rudie Nudie nice and snug.

It wasn't just a book; it was a whole routine. And it was amazing!

'So tell me, what are they doing that is naughty?'

'Every time we read, they get up and run away. We can't get them to stay still or to come back. They're uncontrollable.'

How can you explain to someone who thinks your children are naughty that this is actually a love story that we have come up with together?

'That's not the only thing.'

'Oh really? What else?'

'Every time we pack away, Adelaide pulls everything out again.'

This was a strange one. Very unlike Adelaide. For her, everything had a place, and it had to go back there. It was not like her just to randomly pull things out like that. It was a bit of a mystery. I thought perhaps she was upset about things, or maybe she was angry, or just plain didn't want to do what she was told. Still, it wasn't like my two-year-old Adelaide to pull things out of their place.

The first day I came home to stay, I opened the drawer to look for the wooden train set. 'Let's make the train set, Adelaide.'

We didn't find a wooden train set in the drawer where a wooden train set had always been kept. No. We found a blancmange of bits. There were train tracks and carriages, Lego pieces, fluffy toys, and worst of all, puzzle pieces, random puzzle pieces from all sorts of different places simply shot in the one spot.

Adelaide was on one side of the drawer. I was on the other. It was like the drawer opened in slow motion. I could hear the soundtrack. Adelaide knew what was coming. 'What is going on here?' I half-screamed in horror. We both put our hands to our faces.

Adelaide looked at me. I looked at Adelaide. We looked at the blancmange.

'It's really bad Mummy.' Her head slumped, and her shoulders tightened. She was ashamed of the drawer of stuff that should have been organised but was all over the place.

'Oh, Adelaide. What a mess.' She started to cry. Just very quiet tears, but very real tears. Not the tears of a naughty girl. Two-year-olds don't know how to make a decision to be naughty. They were the tears of someone who knew things weren't right and had not been so for a very long time. 'Let's fix it.'

From Adelaide came a huge inhale of air, and then a rush of breath. She looked at me, and the tears stopped. I could feel her little body say, 'The world will be right.' Her head lifted, her face brightened, and we tackled that dessert. The timber train stayed where it was, the Lego went safely in an enclosed tub where we couldn't tread on it and draw blood, some of the fluffy toys needed to go, and the puzzle pieces found zip-lock bags together with their mates. It was a major feat. We could stand back and admire our work at the end. We deserved a medal.

Adelaide wasn't being naughty. She was trying to make sense of the world when she didn't have a voice to make sense of it. She was making sense the only way she knew how. The problem was, until I came home, no one was listening.

I have always vowed to be the voice for my children. While they need me, I will be their advocate. One day they won't need me so much. I will always be there, but they will need me differently. That will mean I have done my job: it will mean I have taught my children to be independent, to speak for themselves. That is the double-edged sword of a parent: we are teaching them to not really need us. We are teaching them to use their own voices.

My Fight Song

I made a date with Dr Herkes. It was December 2013, just before he closed for Christmas.

It was a hot day. I wore long pants so nothing would rub on my legs. I got there five months after I first met him.

'Well. Look at you!'

He said it like a proud father. He was dressed in a navy-blue suit, like he was ready to go to a school formal.

'How did you get here?'

'I drove!' I said, with the pride of someone who had just achieved their driver's licence for the first time. Except this was my second time.

It felt different seeing him in his office rather than at Royal North Shore. It felt more private, more intimate than when he came visiting without his groupies. This was like coming to his home. He was surrounded by his books and photographs. There were even children's drawings on the wall. I don't know if they were his children's, his grandchildren's, or from children he had cured, children whose lives he had given back to them.

Here he was, a real person with a story around him. In the hospital, he was a demigod. It was easy to see why, I guess, he held people's lives in his hands. He certainly held mine. He saved it. He brought it back from the brink.

He went and sat behind his desk. Like all geniuses, his desk was a bit of a shambles, organised into crazy piles. I'm not critical of the piles; that's how my desk always was at work. If anyone ever asked, 'Where's the blue striped Post-it note with the phone number for the lady who sold the cupcakes at last Tuesday afternoon's information session?' I knew exactly which piece of dog-eared paper it was stuck under! Dr Herkes' piles were like that. He knew exactly where everything was. He was a true genius.

The desk took up the width of his office. Behind me was an examination bed; behind him was a window. The Venetians were pulled closed to block the glare. The light still came through in horizontal lines and, because I was emotional about being there, the light made my eyes water, just a trickle. It gave Dr Herkes a glow. Like a saint. Not a fake glow like in a cheesy movie, but a soft, faint light that seemed to radiate out of his body.

He smiled at me with that half-smile as he ever so slightly tilted his head to the right. 'You're doing so well.' I knew he really meant it. I was a little embarrassed because he was congratulating me, and I didn't feel like I deserved it. He was the one who needed congratulating. He was the one who randomly picked up my file on his way home on the 15th of July; he was the one who thought I was 'an interesting case'; he was the one who took a risk and said he thought I had something even though the tests didn't show anything; and he was the one who treated me based on his gut feeling. He was the one who deserved the thanks.

When I think about it now, though, I deserved it too. Dr Herkes was congratulating me. We had to work together as a team. He knew how hard I had to work. I wasn't expected to be able to walk down that hallway or drive down the Pacific Highway to get to him. A lot of that was sheer hard work and stubborn determination.

Dr Herkes helped me up onto the examination table like he was helping me into a carriage. I sat sideways on the bed with my legs dangling over the edge, ugly, uncontrolled dangling. Then I saw it: the dreaded reflex hammer. I don't even know its real name, but I sure know the effect it had on me, and still has on me. Dr Herkes nearly knocked me across the room with that knee knocker to check the reflexes in my leg. It wasn't a good reaction, in fact, it was a huge overreaction, first the right leg, then the left. He started by resting the hammer against my knee, then ever so slightly taking it off and tapping it against the bone. Whoa! It nearly shot us both into the next room! I hated that tool of torture.

We talked about the challenges of getting around at home and going up and down the steps. Those steps were horrendous. They were frightening. I was scared of those steps, scared of going in and out of our own home. Dr Herkes was scared for me. Genuinely scared.

I talked about my children. I told him how I walked with one on my left and one on my right. I didn't realise until they started preschool, but they were like my little stabilisers, literally and figuratively. They held me up, and they were my reason for getting up and walking again.

'No one understands what's wrong. They just think I'm lazy and should be carrying on as I was before.'

'Of course they don't understand. Remember I told you it would be easier if you could say, "I was hit by a bus." People would understand that. Lots of doctors don't even understand what happened to you.'

'People look at me and think there's nothing wrong. They don't realise my brain works so hard to get the messages to the rest of my body. They don't realise my body works just as hard to get the messages back to my brain. People don't realise I have to concentrate to lift my legs every time I want to walk. They don't realise how hard it is to keep my feet pointing in the same direction. They don't understand how awful it is to turn around and see that I've wet myself or dirtied myself in public. Or how embarrassing it is when someone says, "What's that smell?" when I release wind. I just can't help it.'

'It's because you look like there's nothing wrong. People look at you and you don't look any different. If you were hit by a bus, you'd have a broken leg. You'd be wearing a boot and using crutches. People would say, oh, you poor thing. They'd feel sorry for you.'

He was right. If I'd been hit by a bus, there'd be blood and broken bones. People couldn't see that with me. They just saw someone who looked the same. I was injured on the inside, and I tried so hard to hide it on the outside. For so long I pretended there was nothing wrong. But there was a lot wrong. I wasn't the disabled wife making life difficult for Mike.

I was the strong woman, daughter, mother, and wife. The independent, stubborn one who was not going to accept, "You cannot walk, you will not walk, and this is who you are."

I was the strong woman who would listen when told, "I don't know if this is what you have. I think it's this strange, wild thing. And I need you to trust me so I can treat you straight away. I need to poke a hole in your spine and suck the juice out. You don't know me, but I need you to trust me."

I trusted him. I am the strong woman who knew Dr Herkes would help me. He could be trusted. I knew we could work together. I wasn't going to sit and wait. I was going to do all I could to get up and move. I was going to be the strongest woman, daughter, mother, and wife that I could be.

I might not be the same as I was before, but that didn't mean I was weak.

Dr Herkes saved my life that day, the 15th of July 2013. He was on his way home from work and just happened to think I was an interesting case.

There's no doubt he saved my life.

Ian and the staff at Mt Wilga handed my life back.

And I took it. I grabbed it with both hands, and if I could have run, I would have run. As it was, running wasn't an option. I tried, but it was a bit dangerous. So I grabbed it with both hands and hobbled, with both feet proudly pointing in different directions.

I will be forever grateful.

This is my fight song, and I've still got a lot of fight left in me.

This part of my story started on that Absolutely Ordinary Monday, with Alex and Adelaide, Mum and Dad …

It continues.

www.ingramcontent.com/pod-product-compliance
Lightning Source LLC
Chambersburg PA
CBHW061217070526
44584CB00029B/3873